Finding the way through Mark

Finding the way through Mark

JOHN FENTON

MOWBRAY

Mowbray
A Cassell imprint
Wellington House,
125 Strand,
London
WC2R 0BB

215 Park Avenue South,
New York,
NY 10003

First published 1995

British Library Cataloguing-in-Publication Data
A catalogue record for this book is available from the British Library.

ISBN 0–264–67380–8

Typeset by York House Typographic Ltd
Printed and bound in Great Britain by
Biddles Ltd, Guildford and King's Lynn

To

the Dean and Canons,
staff and congregation
of St George's Cathedral,
Perth, Western Australia

———————✦———————

Contents

Preface

When *Finding the Way Through John* was published by Mowbray in 1988, it was suggested that I should follow it with a companion volume on Mark. It proved far more difficult than I had expected, partly because so much has been written on Mark in the last forty years; partly because Mark presents the commentator with many more problems than John.

It was only when the Very Reverend John Shepherd, the Dean of St George's Cathedral, Perth, Western Australia, invited me to spend May and June 1994 at the Cathedral as Theologian in Residence, so that I was about as far as it is possible to be, on this planet, from Oxford and my books and notes that I was able to write the first draft of this book, with nothing except a Greek Testament and a copy of the Revised English Bible (1989).

I do not know whether anyone will find this way of reading Mark helpful; both as I wrote it in Australia, and as I revised it on my return to England, I was constantly reminded of the words of my teacher, Robert Henry Lightfoot (1883–1953): With Mark, you seldom think that you have come off. Indeed you do not.

I am extremely grateful to John Shepherd for inviting my wife and me to Perth, and for the wonderful two months that we spent there. I am also very grateful to my wife for typing the whole book; to Judith Longman, of Mowbray, for very much help and encouragement; and to the Oxford University Press for permission to print the text of the Revised English Bible.

JOHN FENTON
Oxford
All Souls' Day, 1994

Introduction

We know next to nothing about the author of the book we call 'The Gospel according to Mark', but that does not matter: it does not mean that we cannot understand what he wrote. He concealed himself, not telling us who he was or perhaps even his name, since Mark (Markos) was a common name in the first century, and we cannot even be sure that the original text contained the present title of the book. For convenience, we shall refer to him as Mark, and mean by that nothing more than the author of this gospel.

All we know about him for certain is derived from the book itself, not from the earliest writers who mentioned it, and who were probably as ignorant of the author as we are. They claimed that there was a close connection between him and the apostle Peter, but they lived in times when it was necessary to demonstrate that the earliest Christian writings were by members of the original group of twelve disciples of Jesus or at least by people who had been close to them, or by that other apostle, Paul. It is unsafe to accept this tradition, because there seems to have been more of a gap between the original events and the writer of the gospel than there would have been between Peter and one to whom he might have passed on the information. Mark wrote in Greek, not in Aramaic; Aramaic was the language of Jesus and his disciples, but Mark is writing for people who do not know it, so he provides them with translations into Greek of the Aramaic words he uses. We do not even have the text of the original book that Mark wrote, or that he dictated to a scribe (if that was how he composed it); we have only copies made from earlier copies that were themselves made from yet earlier copies; all of them are different, because no one can copy by hand a piece of any length without making mistakes. It is only thanks to the patient work of textual critics over hundreds of years that we can reconstruct with some certainty, but not always with complete confidence, what the first manuscript of Mark's book will have contained. This original manuscript must have been copied and distributed all round the Mediterranean world in the first century, and was used by writers of other gospels: an enlarged second edition of Mark appeared somewhere on the eastern Mediterranean coast, probably about AD 90; and not long after, another enlarged third edition, perhaps not far from the second. These are the books we now know as Matthew's and Luke's gospels. It is possible that the author of John's gospel, too, knew Mark. And all of this happened, probably, before AD 100. The date of Mark, like the authorship of the book, is disputed, but most writers suggest that it was written around AD 70. There is similar uncertainty about the place where it was written; Rome is usually proposed, but again with very little evidence.

The most extraordinary thing about Mark's gospel is its neglect. For seventeen centuries, from the middle of the second century AD to the middle of the nineteenth, though it was certainly part of the official collection of Christian writings, it was used far less than the other three gospels: there are fewer papyrus fragments of it than of the others; fewer quotations from it in the early (or later) writers; fewer commentaries on it than on the other gospels. It is not hard to see why it was so. The writer of Matthew's gospel had done his work so well: he had copied almost all of Mark, and added an account of the birth of Jesus, of his teaching and of his appearances after his resurrection to the women at the tomb and to the eleven disciples in Galilee; he had composed a book that left the reader in no doubt that God had intervened in the world in the life of Jesus, from virginal conception and a miraculous star at the beginning of the book, to earthquakes and an angel at the end. Moreover, he had shown how Jesus had spoken about his followers as the church, and founded it and given it its instructions. Almost anything that was omitted from Mark in Matthew's gospel was to be found in Luke's; so if one had Matthew's book and Luke's, there was, one would think, no need for Mark – particularly since, before the invention of printing in the fifteenth century, every copy must be made by hand.

Mark lay there, in the Bible, unappreciated, until the early nineteenth century, when interest in it was aroused by the suggestion that it might be the earliest of the four gospels, and the principal source of the other three. Then, in the twentieth century, scholars began to recognize in Mark procedures and devices that were the work of an author: how else could one explain the frequent commands to silence in the book, or the description of the disciples as complete failures? Above all, how else could one explain the ending of the book, with the fear and silence of the women at the tomb, and no re-appearance of Jesus, either in Galilee or in Jerusalem? Mark fell within Gerard Manley Hopkins's definition of 'pied beauty':

All things counter, original, spare, strange.

In spite of, or perhaps because of, its austere and terrifying teaching that the only way into life was through the destruction of the self, it seemed to appeal to late twentieth-century readers more immediately and more directly than any of its three competitors.

The book is a gospel, and, as far as we know, it is the first book that was ever called a gospel. The word had been much used by Paul (both the noun and the verb) of the message he preached, in contrast with what his (Christian) opponents said. It meant good news, and just as Paul knew that a crucified man was no good news to Jews or Greeks, so Mark tells us a story that at first reading must seem extraordinarily sad and tragic: the one central character is rejected by his mother and his brothers, by the Pharisees and the Herodians, and by the scribes from Jerusalem; he is arrested by the authorities from the temple at Jerusalem, condemned for blasphemy and executed by the Romans in mid-day darkness and with mockery from all; none of his male disciples stands by him, only women, at a distance; and when they are told by a young man to take a message to his disciples to say that he is alive, they fail to do so, because they are afraid. How can a story like that be good news?

Mark has deliberately and with great care presented his readers with this problem. There is no easy or superficial answer to the question, Why is Jesus good news? Mark does not want us to think we know. He wants his readers to be absolutely clear that if the book is a gospel, it is not what one might have expected a gospel to be. There is violence, conflict, destruction, from beginning to end; and it is possible that this has contributed to the neglect of the book. A sixteenth-century Spanish writer said of Mark, chapter 8, that the more necessary its teaching was, the less it was practised. Mark is a book that tells us what we do not want to hear. It belongs to a Jewish–Christian school of writers (e.g. Daniel, 2 Thessalonians, Revelation) who believed that things must get worse before they get better. Mark's purpose is to instil in his readers the necessity of accepting the worse, and the hope that there will be a better.

1.1–13 Mark's introduction

The beginning of the gospel of Jesus Christ the Son of God.

[2] In the prophet Isaiah it stands written:

I am sending my herald ahead of you;
he will prepare your way.
[3] A voice cries in the wilderness,
'Prepare the way for the Lord;
clear a straight path for him.'

[4] John the Baptist appeared in the wilderness proclaiming a baptism in token of repentance, for the forgiveness of sins; [5] and everyone flocked to him from the countryside of Judaea and the city of Jerusalem, and they were baptized by him in the river Jordan, confessing their sins. [6] John was dressed in a rough coat of camel's hair, with a leather belt round his waist, and he fed on locusts and wild honey. [7] He proclaimed: 'After me comes one mightier than I am, whose sandals I am not worthy to stoop down and unfasten. [8] I have baptized you with water; he will baptize you with the Holy Spirit.'
[9] It was at this time that Jesus came from Nazareth in Galilee and was baptized in the Jordan by John. [10] As he was coming up out of the water, he saw the heavens break open and the Spirit descend on him, like a dove. [11] And a voice came from heaven: 'You are my beloved Son; in you I take delight.'
[12] At once the Spirit drove him out into the wilderness, [13] and there he remained for forty days tempted by Satan. He was among the wild beasts; and angels attended to his needs.

The beginnings and the endings of books are the most difficult parts to write; their function is to admit the readers to the text and dismiss them at the end of it. Mark's conclusion to his book is notoriously abrupt, and was felt to be so from the first; his opening paragraphs are similar, and none of his revisers left them untouched.

The ideas are rich and densely packed. There are two chief characters, John the Baptist and Jesus. John's message is Repent, be baptized, receive forgiveness, because there is one coming who is of far greater importance than him, just as God's Spirit surpasses water in its effect.

But already Mark has brought other persons to our attention: Isaiah the prophet has been quoted explicitly, and, though his name has not been mentioned, so has another prophet, Malachi. Moreover, yet a third prophet is involved in the preparation for the arrival of Jesus in the area of the river Jordan: John is Elijah, who had been taken up to heaven alive, and has now returned; his clothes are his identification (2 Kings 1.8).

We are thus left in no doubt that the age to come of which the prophets had spoken is now drawing near, and the promise that God would pour out his Spirit will soon be fulfilled. The Baptist arouses our expectations, and we are not disappointed, because the Spirit comes upon Jesus and a voice from heaven declares him to be God's one and only Son, in whom he delights. Nevertheless, in typically Marcan fashion, we are not allowed to pause there; continual movement is a characteristic of this book. The Spirit forces Jesus out into the wilderness, where he is tested by Satan over a period of forty days, in the mixed company of wild beasts and angels, and it will only be later (3.27) that we shall be told that he has bound Satan in order to release the world from his tyranny.

These first thirteen verses introduce all the elements that are needed for understanding what is to follow in the rest of the book. The Baptist is the herald, Elijah, who is to prepare for the Lord by announcing forgiveness through repentance and baptism. Jesus is the unique Son of God, the agent in whom God delights, who will overthrow Satan and bring to the world the greatest gift that it is possible for humans to receive, the Spirit of God; that is, participation in the life of the creator and source of all existence. Jesus receives the Spirit, in order that he may do God's will and distribute the Spirit to others. But this will involve him in conflict and in overcoming opposition to the will of God, and this is hinted at by the references to Satan, temptation and the wild beasts in the wilderness. Mark draws our attention to the struggle that is taking place between Jesus and Satan, and says nothing that might distract us from it: there is nothing to say that Jesus fasted, or what form the temptations took (as in Matthew and Luke), nor even, at this point, what the outcome was. Mark knows that faith in God's power to overcome evil is tested in darkness and desolation, and he does nothing to alleviate the ambiguity of the way in which the disciple follows Christ, or indeed of the way that Jesus goes ahead to destroy and be destroyed.

1.14–45   The rule of God

[14] After John had been arrested, Jesus came into Galilee proclaiming the gospel of God: [15] 'The time has arrived; the kingdom of God is upon you. Repent, and believe the gospel.'

[16] Jesus was walking by the sea of Galilee when he saw Simon and his brother Andrew at work with casting-nets in the lake; for they were fishermen. [17] Jesus said to them, 'Come, follow me, and I will make you fishers of men.' [18] At once they left their nets and followed him.

[19] Going a little farther, he saw James son of Zebedee and his brother John in a boat mending their nets. [20] At once he called them; and they left their father Zebedee in the boat with the hired men and followed him.

[21] They came to Capernaum, and on the sabbath he went to the synagogue and began to teach. [22] The people were amazed at his teaching, for, unlike the scribes, he taught with a note of authority. [23] Now there was a man in their synagogue possessed by an unclean spirit. He shrieked at him: [24] 'What do you want with us, Jesus of Nazareth? Have you come to destroy us? I know who you are – the Holy One of God.' [25] Jesus rebuked him: 'Be silent', he said, 'and come out of him.' [26] The unclean spirit threw the man into convulsions and with a loud cry left him. [27] They were all amazed and began to ask one another, 'What is this? A new kind of teaching! He speaks with

authority. When he gives orders, even the unclean spirits obey.' ²⁸ His fame soon spread far and wide throughout Galilee.

²⁹ On leaving the synagogue, they went straight to the house of Simon and Andrew; and James and John went with them. ³⁰ Simon's mother-in-law was in bed with a fever. As soon as they told him about her, ³¹ Jesus went and took hold of her hand, and raised her to her feet. The fever left her, and she attended to their needs.

³² That evening after sunset they brought to him all who were ill or possessed by demons; ³³ and the whole town was there, gathered at the door. ³⁴ He healed many who suffered from various diseases, and drove out many demons. He would not let the demons speak, because they knew who he was.

³⁵ Very early next morning he got up and went out. He went away to a remote spot and remained there in prayer. ³⁶ But Simon and his companions went in search of him, ³⁷ and when they found him, they said, 'Everybody is looking for you.' ³⁸ He answered, 'Let us move on to the neighbouring towns, so that I can proclaim my message there as well, for that is what I came out to do.' ³⁹ So he went through the whole of Galilee, preaching in their synagogues and driving out demons.

⁴⁰ On one occasion he was approached by a leper, who knelt before him and begged for help. 'If only you will,' said the man, 'you can make me clean.' ⁴¹ Jesus was moved to anger; he stretched out his hand, touched him, and said, 'I will; be clean.' ⁴² The leprosy left him immediately, and he was clean. ⁴³ Then he dismissed him with this stern warning: ⁴⁴ 'See that you tell nobody, but go and show yourself to the priest, and make the offering laid down by Moses for your cleansing; that will certify the cure.' ⁴⁵ But the man went away and made the whole story public, spreading it far and wide, until Jesus could no longer show himself in any town. He stayed outside in remote places; yet people kept coming to him from all quarters.

Sometimes Mark writes 'good news concerning Jesus': that he is God's Son and that God delights in him; he will be good news for us, because he will baptize us with the Holy Spirit. But here Mark writes 'good news of God': the time has come when he will begin to rule the world, both in heaven and on earth. Evil will be banished, and it will be possible for human beings to share in the blessings of the new age.

Mark's understanding is that we live in a world that is almost completely controlled by evil, and that this evil will have to be destroyed before God's rule can begin, and his will be done. The characteristic mark of evil is its destructiveness, making people ill and crippled, making the earth a place of hunger and danger and death. Evil, that is to say, is parasitic: it lives off what God has created; Satan cannot make, he can only spoil what God has made. The destroyer and his minions, the demons or unclean spirits, will have to be destroyed in order that God's kingdom may come; and, immediately after his encounter with Satan in the wilderness and the arrest of John the Baptist, Jesus announces that the time has come for this to happen. (John is handed over to destruction, just as Jesus will be handed over to be eliminated by those who rule the world; this is, in Mark's mind, the way it must be: gain comes through loss, and salvation through destruction.) To accept the good news of God, all that is needed is repentance and faith, changing one's mind from the way human beings think, and believing that what seems impossible is in fact the way God works.

The authors of gospels have taken great care to present the first words of Jesus in their books in a form that summarizes his whole message as they understand it; and this is why each gospel is different from the others in what is put into the mouth of Jesus as his opening words. Mark's firmest conviction is that God will make well all that is not well; he will act so that his name will be honoured, his rule on the earth will begin and his will only be done. The expression 'the kingdom of God' will come fourteen times in Mark's book, thirteen of them in the words of Jesus, and once, after his death, in a comment made by Mark (15.43). It refers throughout to the time, after the last judgement, when the world will be brought under God's direct and immediate rule. One can trace the origin of the expression back to the writer of Daniel, the last book of the Old Testament, written in the second century BC. After the four great empires of the Babylonians,

Medes, Persians and Greeks, there would be a kingdom that did not end; those empires were symbolized by beasts, the final kingdom by one who was like a human being (Daniel 2 and 7). History is a downhill progress, and God intervenes when the lowest level has been reached.

It is significant which incident Mark puts next in his account of the ministry of Jesus. We might have expected that it would be an exorcism, since he is so well supplied with stories of that sort, and they were much to his liking. But it is not so; the first incident, he decides, is to be the calling of disciples to follow Jesus and the promise that he will make them fishers of men. Jesus associates people with himself, and that is his first action in the book. He will say of those who pay attention to him, that they are his family; he will speak of them as his own, and refer to them as the elect, those whom God has chosen; they will be gathered by his angels into the new age, when he comes to judge the world and to establish God's kingdom on the earth. Mark will not allow his readers to forget the cost of such discipleship: the fishermen must leave their occupation and their families, if they are to be followers; those who have given up everything will be rewarded with eternal life in the age to come. But that is not where the emphasis is being placed by the priority given to the invitation to follow Jesus; rather, it is the extraordinary fact that Jesus chooses companions, and that God desires company.

The first exorcism comes next, in the synagogue at Capernaum. It is unique in this gospel because it is the only occasion on which an unclean spirit is cast out in a synagogue. Two themes are wound together, Jesus and Judaism, and Jesus and evil. He confronts the synagogue congregation with new teaching, and the possessed man with authority and power. The spirit speaks first, shouting out that there is nothing in common between the forces of evil and Jesus of Nazareth; the two sides are utterly opposed to one another, one being set on destruction and the other on salvation. The spirit has understanding, beyond that of flesh and blood. He knows what Jesus has come to do: he has

10

come to destroy him and his colleagues; he will destroy those who destroy the earth. He also knows who Jesus is: the Holy One of God, who has no trace of evil in him. But what he does not know is the manner in which he will be destroyed, and because he does not know this, he is silenced. The cure of the possessed man is described: the spirit convulses him and comes out with a loud cry; evil is tenacious, and can only be dealt with in a bitter struggle; Jesus too will utter a loud cry as he dies. The comments of the congregation point to what can be seen and heard: New teaching, authority of a different kind from that of the scribes, the overthrow of the powers of darkness.

Mark, like Paul before him, sees the law of Moses as a power that must be removed because it prevents us from being free and restricts our liberty. The law creates divisions into Jews and gentiles, slaves and free, males and females. Jesus has come to end that and break down barriers. Satan and Judaism line up against him. He will destroy them, by being destroyed by them. But this is what no one in the narrative knows yet, except Jesus; so he silences the unclean spirit, whose true prediction, You have come to destroy us, is only part of the truth. Those who read Mark, however, and know how the story as a whole will end, are able to appreciate the drollness of the situation that here is a knowing spirit who knows only half the truth.

The healing in the synagogue described the destruction of the opposition and emphasized the negative aspect of Christ's work; nothing was said on the positive side about the health and sanity of the man who had previously been possessed. The healing of Peter's mother-in-law expresses the positive aspect, in that she is raised up from her fever-bed and enabled to serve the sabbath meal.

Exorcism and healing, however, are only signs of God's coming rule; they point to the presence of a power that is stronger than Satan's, but they do not and cannot show how this power will be exercised, and what will be done to rid the world of destruction.

The demons know who Jesus is, but that is all they know; they know that he is their destroyer, but not how he will overcome them. They too are silenced, because their testimony is inadequate, incomplete, and therefore misleading.

The ambiguity of the situation is emphasized further by the decision of Jesus to leave Capernaum at the height of his popularity, when everybody was seeking him for the wrong reason, and to go to the neighbouring towns to preach there, and to continue to perform the signs of the coming rule of God by casting out demons.

The cure of the man with the skin disease (not, apparently, what is meant today by leprosy) illustrates the problem of miracles and their relationship to the gospel. Paul had said, Jews demand miracles, but we preach Christ crucified, which is no miracle but rather the absence of miracle; therefore it is a stumbling-block to Jews. Miracle stories illustrate the effect that Jesus has: he removes destructiveness, makes mad people sane, replaces uncleanness with holiness; but they suggest a procedure that is an act of power, whereas salvation is through weakness, suffering and being destroyed. The leper is tempting Jesus: If only you will, you can make me clean. He is healed, with the command that he tells nobody but goes through the prescribed procedure for the certification of a cure. He does not do what he is told, with the result that Jesus can do no more cures in towns. Healings, or any other miracles, if they are not used as signs but are treated as the reality, can only mislead.

Miracle stories are more frequent in the pages of Mark than in those of any of the other evangelists. Nevertheless, Mark is not unaware of the problem that they raise. This can be seen from the arrangement of the miracle stories in his book: fifteen of the eighteen miracles described in detail are in the first half of the gospel; the nearer we are to Jerusalem, and to Golgotha in particular, the fewer the miracles. Salvation will not be by miraculous deliverance from evil, but by the destruction of the saviour, because anyone who saves his life will destroy it.

2.1 – 3.6   The gospel and the law

After some days he returned to Capernaum, and news went round that he was at home; [2] and such a crowd collected that there was no room for them even in the space outside the door. While he was proclaiming the message to them, [3] a man was brought who was paralysed. Four men were carrying him, [4] but because of the crowd they could not get him near. So they made an opening in the roof over the place where Jesus was, and when they had broken through they lowered the bed on which the paralysed man was lying. [5] When he saw their faith, Jesus said to the man, 'My son, your sins are forgiven.'
[6] Now there were some scribes sitting there, thinking to themselves, [7] 'How can the fellow talk like that? It is blasphemy! Who but God can forgive sins?' [8] Jesus knew at once what they were thinking, and said to them, 'Why do you harbour such thoughts? [9] Is it easier to say to this paralysed man, "Your sins are forgiven," or to say, "Stand up, take your bed, and walk"? [10] But to convince you that the Son of Man has authority on earth to forgive sins' – he turned to the paralysed man – [11] 'I say to you, stand up, take your bed, and go home.' [12] And he got up, and at once took his bed and went out in full view of them all, so that they were astounded and praised God. 'Never before', they said, 'have we seen anything like this.'
[13] Once more he went out to the lakeside. All the crowd came to him there, and he taught them. [14] As he went along, he saw Levi son of Alphaeus at his seat in the custom-house, and said to him, 'Follow me'; and he rose and followed him.
[15] When Jesus was having a meal in his house, many tax-collectors and sinners were seated with him and his disciples, for there were many of them among his followers. [16] Some scribes who were Pharisees, observing the company in which he was eating, said to his disciples, 'Why does he eat with tax-collectors and sinners?' [17] Hearing this, Jesus said to them, 'It is not the healthy who need a doctor, but the sick; I did not come to call the virtuous, but sinners.'
[18] Once, when John's disciples and the Pharisees were keeping a fast, some people came and asked him, 'Why is it that John's disciples and the disciples of the Pharisees are fasting, but yours are not?' [19] Jesus replied, 'Can you expect the bridegroom's friends to fast while the bridegroom is with them? As long as he is with them, there can be no

fasting. [20] But the time will come when the bridegroom will be taken away from them; that will be the time for them to fast.

[21] 'No one sews a patch of unshrunk cloth on to an old garment; if he does, the patch tears away from it, the new from the old, and leaves a bigger hole. [22] No one puts new wine into old wineskins; if he does, the wine will burst the skins, and then wine and skins are both lost. New wine goes into fresh skins.'

[23] One sabbath he was going through the cornfields; and as they went along his disciples began to pluck ears of corn. [24] The Pharisees said to him, 'Why are they doing what is forbidden on the sabbath?' [25] He answered, 'Have you never read what David did when he and his men were hungry and had nothing to eat? [26] He went into the house of God, in the time of Abiathar the high priest, and ate the sacred bread, though no one but a priest is allowed to eat it, and even gave it to his men.'

[27] He also said to them, 'The sabbath was made for man, not man for the sabbath: [28] so the Son of Man is lord even of the sabbath.'

3 On another occasion when he went to synagogue, there was a man in the congregation who had a withered arm; [2] and they were watching to see whether Jesus would heal him on the sabbath, so that they could bring a charge against him. [3] He said to the man with the withered arm, 'Come and stand out here.' [4] Then he turned to them: 'Is it permitted to do good or to do evil on the sabbath, to save life or to kill?' They had nothing to say; [5] and, looking round at them with anger and sorrow at their obstinate stupidity, he said to the man, 'Stretch out your arm.' He stretched it out and his arm was restored. [6] Then the Pharisees, on leaving the synagogue, at once began plotting with the men of Herod's party to bring about Jesus's death.

Mark now puts before his readers a collection of stories that are linked together by one theme running through each of them. In every case, there is conflict between the representatives of Judaism on one side, and Jesus and his disciples on the other. The thread that holds these stories together is the opposition between those who keep the law of Moses and those who believe the good news; and the climax of the series is reached in the final incident, when the Pharisees and the party of Herod decide to destroy Jesus.

Mark believed that everything that he wrote about in his book was the direct result of the action of God; though God's voice is heard only twice, at the baptism and at the transfiguration, he is, Mark believes, the source of all the action, just as his will eventually be the one and only purpose that is effective. Three times Mark has the phrase, Nothing is impossible – to God, or to the person who believes in God.

But what becomes abundantly clear as Mark's book proceeds is that the activity of God is surprising, unexpected and contrary to what anyone else would do. The doings of God are wonderful in our eyes because they are so unlike our doings. Mark draws our attention to this, in the middle of this section of his book: no one, Jesus says, would patch an old garment with new cloth; no one would put new wine into old skins. If we did, there would be a larger hole in the garment and the wine and the skins would both be destroyed. Yet this is exactly what God does: he brings Jesus with the gospel into Judaism, the new into the old; what will happen is what you would expect: the old will destroy the new (Jesus will be put to death), and the new will destroy the old (Judaism will become outmoded). The conflict, therefore, between the representatives of the law and Jesus is intense, and will issue in destruction for both (and in the resurrection of Jesus, God's final act).

In the account of the healing of the paralysed man, Mark reveals the totally unexpected freedom of God to forgive. Nothing is said about the state of the man's mind. Was he penitent? Was he worthy? All we are told about is the persistence of his companions, who go so far as to dig up the roof of the house and lower the sick man into the presence of Jesus. It is a kind of funeral, seen from an unusual angle. To die with Christ is also to live with him. Jesus is not a blasphemer, as the scribes suppose. The healing is evidence of the reality of the forgiveness and of Jesus' authority to declare, what the Baptist had already declared, that God has forgiven sins, and that all that is needed is

15

the faith to accept this by repenting. The good news provokes two, contrary, reactions: in the scribes, that Jesus is wicked; in others, that it is too good to be true, but even so we shall believe it.

Mark has arranged the stories in this series in such a way that the opposition to Jesus develops, and becomes more intense and more focused on Jesus, as one incident follows another. In the first story, the scribes thought that Jesus was blaspheming, and he read their thoughts and interpreted them to them. In the second story, they complain to his disciples about the company he keeps, eating with sinners, and Jesus answers with the first parable in this gospel: he is the doctor, and it is right that the doctor should be found with the sick; he has invited sinners to his table, not the virtuous. The gospel is biased in favour of the wicked; the advantage they have is that they will be more likely to repent. The problem with the law, as Paul had found, is that one might keep it, and that would make repentance unnecessary.

In the third incident, the question is put to Jesus directly, but it is a question about the behaviour of his disciples; they are not fasting when the followers of the Baptist and of the Pharisees are. His answer is another parable; like the parable of the doctor, this one, about the bridegroom, implies some kind of claim for himself, that he is not as others are; he is a special person, of unique status (as we have heard at the beginning of the book, the voice from heaven has called him his beloved Son), and in his presence even the law of Moses gives way. At this point we are told for the first time that there will be a day when he will be taken away; Jesus predicts his death shortly before his opponents plot it. He is always ahead of them; and whatever they do, it will be according to God's will and purpose.

In the fourth story, about the sabbath in the cornfields, it is again the behaviour of the disciples that is the cause of the conflict, and again Jesus defends them with the same argument. David and his companions broke the law about the sacred bread in the house of God; the disciples can break the sabbath law, because Jesus is greater than the sabbath, and in his presence law is replaced by freedom.

In the fifth and final element in this series, the opposition fixes its attention on Jesus himself: Will he heal on the sabbath? His answer poses the question, What is permitted on the sabbath? Is it a day for doing good, and saving life, or a day for doing evil and killing? There is always danger when Jesus asks a question, and his opponents on this occasion fail to avoid it. He saves life and does good; they plan to kill him and do evil. Which of them is keeping the sabbath?

Twice over in this group of stories Jesus refers to himself as the Son of Man. It is an expression that will be used again, and more frequently, in the later part of the book, and it will always come in the direct speech of Jesus; nobody refers to him as the Son of Man. Once again, it is possible that the use of the expression by Christian writers owes something to their reading of the book of Daniel. The one whom Daniel saw in his dream, like a human being, was, literally, a son of man (Daniel 7.13), and Mark and the other writers of gospels believed that Jesus had used this as a title, which applied to himself. They believed that Jesus would come again at the end of world-history, to judge everybody and establish God's rule on the earth; and they believed that this would happen soon. Jesus, they said, had lived and taught a new kind of life, one that was free from limitations and restrictions, and that disregarded the divisions that religious laws created (holy/unholy; clean/unclean). His freedom was appreciated best by those who did not belong to a religious system; those who had dropped out, or been excluded.

His behaviour, and that of his followers, inevitably provoked deadly opposition from those who were the official representatives of the system and whose function was, they believed, to enforce it. Freedom and the yoke of slavery are mutually exclusive alternatives, diametrically opposed to each other.

Mark's readers can now anticipate the rest of his narrative, including the death of Jesus; and, if they attend to the expression, the Son of Man, they may also look forward to God's final action in establishing his rule on the earth, and with it the freedom that is his will and his gift.

3.7–35   Companions and opponents

⁷ Jesus went away to the lakeside with his disciples. Great numbers from Galilee, Judaea ⁸ and Jerusalem, Idumaea and Transjordan, and the neighbourhood of Tyre and Sidon, heard what he was doing and came to him. ⁹ So he told his disciples to have a boat ready for him, to save him from being crushed by the crowd. ¹⁰ For he healed so many that the sick all came crowding round to touch him. ¹¹ The unclean spirits too, when they saw him, would fall at his feet and cry aloud, 'You are the Son of God'; ¹² but he insisted that they should not make him known.

¹³ Then he went up into the hill-country and summoned the men he wanted; and they came and joined him. ¹⁴ He appointed twelve to be his companions, and to be sent out to proclaim the gospel, ¹⁵ with authority to drive out demons. ¹⁶ The Twelve he appointed were: Simon, whom he named Peter; ¹⁷ the sons of Zebedee, James and his brother John, whom he named Boanerges, Sons of Thunder; ¹⁸ Andrew, Philip, Bartholomew, Matthew, Thomas, James son of Alphaeus, Thaddaeus, Simon the Zealot, ¹⁹ and Judas Iscariot, the man who betrayed him.

He entered a house, ²⁰ and once more such a crowd collected round them that they had no chance even to eat. ²¹ When his family heard about it they set out to take charge of him. 'He is out of his mind,' they said.

²² The scribes, too, who had come down from Jerusalem, said, 'He is possessed by Beelzebul,' and, 'He drives out demons by the prince of demons.' ²³ So he summoned them, and spoke to them in parables: 'How can Satan drive out Satan? ²⁴ If a kingdom is divided against itself, that kingdom cannot stand; ²⁵ if a household is divided against itself, that house cannot stand; ²⁶ and if Satan is divided and rebels against himself, he cannot stand, and that is the end of him.

27 'On the other hand, no one can break into a strong man's house and make off with his goods unless he has first tied up the strong man; then he can ransack the house.

28 'Truly I tell you: every sin and every slander can be forgiven; 29 but whoever slanders the Holy Spirit can never be forgiven; he is guilty of an eternal sin.' 30 He said this because they had declared that he was possessed by an unclean spirit.

31 Then his mother and his brothers arrived; they stayed outside and sent in a message asking him to come out to them. 32 A crowd was sitting round him when word was brought that his mother and brothers were outside asking for him. 33 'Who are my mother and my brothers?' he replied. 34 And looking round at those who were sitting in the circle about him he said, 'Here are my mother and my brothers. 35 Whoever does the will of God is my brother and sister and mother.'

The section begins with another account of a mistaken response to Jesus. Crowds come from all over, but they are attracted by the healings; and the unclean spirits declare him to be the Son of God. Jesus silences them, because their knowledge of him is so incomplete as to be misleading. The good news is not about life, but about life through death.

What determines membership of the company of Jesus is not the belief that he is a healer, a miracle worker, the powerful Son of God; unclean spirits can believe that, and shudder. What determines membership of his company is his own call, summons and appointment. Mark gives us a list of twelve, signifying the reformed Israel of twelvefold completion. But even here, the oddness of God's ways is not lost sight of, because one of the Twelve is the man who will hand Jesus over to death.

No one should presume upon the call of Jesus, the invitation to follow him. Those who are closest to him physically are not thereby included among his followers; in fact, they are, Mark says, on the other side, and are part of the opposition to him. His family thinks he is mad and sets out to arrest him. (Mark will use the same word again when Jesus is arrested for execution in Gethsemane: 14.44, 46, 49.) When they arrive, we are told that they are not his mother, his brothers or his sisters, because they do not do the will of God. Those who do God's will are those who are sitting in a circle around Jesus. It is being with him that counts, not being a relation by birth; and being with him is the result of his decision and invitation; in Mark, nobody volunteers to follow Jesus.

Mark inserts the account of the scribes from Jerusalem into the story of the family's unbelief; the two groups share much the same point of view. The scribes say that Jesus is in the power of Beelzebul, that is, Satan. Jesus answers them in parables: If this were so and Satan were divided and working against himself, then that would mean that the time of his sovereignty was coming to an end. And that is, in fact, the case, though the scribes do not know it; and for a different reason than that which they suppose. They have reached the right conclusion by means of a wrong argument. The truth of the matter is that Jesus has tied up Satan, the strong man in the parable, and is making off with his goods, the sick, the possessed and all whom Satan has afflicted. The healings and the exorcisms are evidence that Satan has been overcome. Jesus had been with him in the wilderness, and now we are told the result. We should, no doubt, have seen it for ourselves, earlier on, when Jesus commanded an unclean spirit and it obeyed him and came out. All such spirits and demons have now lost their power.

Jesus could overcome Satan because God's Spirit had come upon him when he was baptized. To call this Holy Spirit an unclean spirit is to call good, evil; not even the demons do that: they know who he really is, the Holy One of God, God's Son. The scribes from Jerusalem are doing what the Pharisees and Herodians had done when they planned to destroy the one who gave life on the sabbath. The most serious sin, the sin that can never be forgiven, Mark says, is the sin of the mind that is confused in its thinking. Mark will return to the subject later, when he says that the source of uncleanness is the mind that thinks evil thoughts.

Certainly Jesus is an anomaly, and does not fit into any of the established categories. This is the starting-point: the voice from heaven said he was the only Son. To say that he is not an anomaly, but that he is yet another charlatan, the most recent in the long list of those who have used power for their own purposes, is not to think straight; it would perhaps be slightly less mistaken to think him mad, with his family, than to think him bad, with the scribes. For them, and for those who think like them, Mark can offer no hope.

4.1–34 Insiders and outsiders

On another occasion he began to teach by the lakeside. The crowd that gathered round him was so large that he had to get into a boat on the lake and sit there, with the whole crowd on the beach right down to the water's edge. [2] And he taught them many things by parables. As he taught he said:

[3] 'Listen! A sower went out to sow. [4] And it happened that as he sowed, some of the seed fell along the footpath; and the birds came and ate it up. [5] Some fell on rocky ground, where it had little soil, and it sprouted quickly because it had no depth of earth; [6] but when the sun rose it was scorched, and as it had no root it withered away. [7] Some fell among thistles; and the thistles grew up and choked the corn, and it produced no crop. [8] And some of the seed fell into good soil, where it came up and grew, and produced a crop; and the yield was thirtyfold, sixtyfold, even a hundredfold.' [9] He added, 'If you have ears to hear, then hear.'

[10] When Jesus was alone with the Twelve and his other companions they questioned him about the parables. [11] He answered, 'To you the secret of the kingdom of God has been given; but to those who are outside, everything comes by way of parables, [12] so that (as scripture says) they may look and look, but see nothing; they may listen and listen, but understand nothing; otherwise they might turn to God and be forgiven.'

[13] He went on: 'Do you not understand this parable? How then are you to understand any parable? [14] The sower sows the word. [15] With some the seed falls along the footpath; no sooner have they heard it than Satan comes and carries off the word which has been sown in

them. [16] With others the seed falls on rocky ground; as soon as they hear the word, they accept it with joy, [17] but it strikes no root in them; they have no staying-power, and when there is trouble or persecution on account of the word, they quickly lose faith. [18] With others again the seed falls among thistles; they hear the word, [19] but worldly cares and the false glamour of wealth and evil desires of all kinds come in and choke the word, and it proves barren. [20] But there are some with whom the seed is sown on good soil; they accept the word when they hear it, and they bear fruit thirtyfold, sixtyfold, or a hundredfold.'

[21] He said to them, 'Is a lamp brought in to be put under the measuring bowl or under the bed? No, it is put on the lampstand. [22] Nothing is hidden except to be disclosed, and nothing concealed except to be brought into the open. [23] If you have ears to hear, then hear.'

[24] He also said to them, 'Take note of what you hear; the measure you give is the measure you will receive, with something more besides. [25] For those who have will be given more, and those who have not will forfeit even what they have.'

[26] He said, 'The kingdom of God is like this. A man scatters seed on the ground; [27] he goes to bed at night and gets up in the morning, and meanwhile the seed sprouts and grows – how, he does not know. [28] The ground produces a crop by itself, first the blade, then the ear, then full grain in the ear; [29] but as soon as the crop is ripe, he starts reaping, because harvest time has come.'

[30] He said, 'How shall we picture the kingdom of God, or what parable shall we use to describe it? [31] It is like a mustard seed; when sown in the ground it is smaller than any other seed, [32] but once sown, it springs up and grows taller than any other plant, and forms branches so large that birds can roost in its shade.'

[33] With many such parables he used to give them his message, so far as they were able to receive it. [34] He never spoke to them except in parables; but privately to his disciples he explained everything.

There have already been two occasions on which Mark has turned to parables in order to explain his narrative; the first was the doctor and the bridegroom, the patch and the wineskins, in chapter 2; the second was the strong man bound, in chapter 3. Now, a further problem faces the reader, and more and longer parables are provided in order to point towards a solution.

The problem here is, Why do some people believe, while others do not? And since this is what happens, how can God's kingdom ever come on the earth, if the number of those who believe and accept his will is so small?

The boat, which Jesus had told his disciples to have ready for him, is now used as the place from which he teaches, on the lake; and the crowd, which had been crushing him, is on the land, at the water's edge. This literal separation between the teacher and the taught is the subject of the sayings that follow, and their purpose is to explain it.

The parable of the sower, the seed and the different kinds of ground works by exaggeration. Three-quarters of the parable deal with seed that bears no fruit, and only one quarter with seed that is fruitful; yet the one quarter that is fruitful produces, at worst, thirty times as much as was sown on the good soil, more than enough to make up for what was wasted. Both failure and success are exaggerated; the parable distorts the facts to make its point, which is that in agriculture fruitfulness exceeds waste and farming is profitable in spite of apparent losses on the way.

The saying which is added after the parable, If you have ears to hear, then hear, makes use of the very problem that the parable is explaining. Some people hear and understand, while others do not. Those who can are exhorted to do so. This is how it is with the hearing of the gospel, just as it is how it is with sowing and soil. To see only the failure is to miss the total result. The parable invites the hearers to change the way that they look, from concentrating on the unbelief of many, to realizing that there is faith and that the believers make up for the others, in a sense which is not yet explained.

The parable of the sower and the different kinds of ground illustrates what Mark believes to be the fundamental gospel-truth, that gain is through loss, success through failure, salvation through destruction and life through death.

The Twelve and the other companions of Jesus do not understand this, and never will, right up to the end of the book. The readers of Mark, or the congregation to which the gospel is being read, will understand. They are the insiders, those who attend to Jesus, and they have been given the secret of how God will bring in his rule on earth and include people in his kingdom. Outsiders see only loss, failure, destruction and death.

The parable of the sower is then expounded with one particular application which bears on the narrative of the gospel and explains the apparent failure of Jesus to persuade some of his contemporaries (his family, for example, and those who had come from Jerusalem) to believe in him. Unbelievers are the unproductive ground; to think that they constitute any objection to the truth of what he is saying is as mistaken as to think that seeds that fail to grow are a reason for abandoning agriculture.

The same point is made again by means of the parable of the lamp. No one would bring a lamp into a room in order to put it in a place where it would give no light. But God has, apparently, done this, since Jesus is being rejected by his family and by the authorities from the capital. His message is hidden from them, and concealed. They do not have the ears that hear. Nevertheless, there must be more to God's purpose than meets the eye.

To be able to see and hear and believe is a gift from God, and like all gifts it is to be accepted with thanksgiving; it is certainly not to be presumed upon. God will increase the understanding of those who attend to what they have already received, but gifts that are neglected will cause the deterioration of those who had received them, as was the case with the seeds that failed to bear fruit.

What happens to the fruitful seed is a mystery, and the sower does not know what it is that turns them into stalks with ears of corn on them. Moreover, the field must be reaped in order that the harvest may be gathered. Faith is a strange activity, and there will be terrible events before the Son of Man comes and sends out his angels to gather the elect.

The final parable in this group contrasts small and great: small seed with large plant, small beginnings with the worldwide empire of God in the age to come. Nothing that happens is to make the disciples stop praying for God to rule, or to think that he will not do so.

The final two sentences (verses 33 and 34) are difficult to make sense of; they seem to combine two ideas. One is that the good news is always beyond our ability to understand it. The other is that enough light is given for us to believe that there is something to be understood. What we can make sense of in the gospel never ceases to come to us as a gift; it is always newly seen, something understood.

The difficulty that the reader has in making sense of this section of Mark's book is an example of what is being said here; and this extension of the subject matter into the character of the book is entirely Marcan. He believes it is not possible to speak clearly about that which is not clear, and he does not try to do so.

4.35 – 6.6a   Faith and fear

³⁵ That day, in the evening, he said to them, 'Let us cross over to the other side of the lake.' ³⁶ So they left the crowd and took him with them in the boat in which he had been sitting; and some other boats went with him. ³⁷ A fierce squall blew up and the waves broke over the boat until it was all but swamped. ³⁸ Now he was in the stern asleep on a cushion; they roused him and said, 'Teacher, we are sinking! Do you not care?' ³⁹ He awoke and rebuked the wind, and said to the sea, 'Silence! Be still!' The wind dropped and there was a dead calm. ⁴⁰ He said to them, 'Why are you such cowards? Have you no faith even now?' ⁴¹ They were awestruck and said to one another, 'Who can this be? Even the wind and the sea obey him.'

5 So they came to the country of the Gerasenes on the other side of the lake. ² As he stepped ashore, a man possessed by an unclean spirit came up to him from among the tombs ³ where he had made his home. Nobody could control him any longer; even chains were useless, ⁴ for he had often been fettered and chained up, but had

snapped his chains and broken the fetters. No one was strong enough to master him. [5] Unceasingly, night and day, he would cry aloud among the tombs and on the hillsides and gash himself with stones. [6] When he saw Jesus in the distance, he ran up and flung himself down before him, [7] shouting at the top of his voice, 'What do you want with me, Jesus, son of the Most High God? In God's name do not torment me.' [8] For Jesus was already saying to him, 'Out, unclean spirit, come out of the man!' [9] Jesus asked him, 'What is your name?' 'My name is Legion,' he said, 'there are so many of us.' [10] And he implored Jesus not to send them out of the district. [11] There was a large herd of pigs nearby, feeding on the hillside, [12] and the spirits begged him, 'Send us among the pigs; let us go into them.' [13] He gave them leave; and the unclean spirits came out and went into the pigs; and the herd, of about two thousand, rushed over the edge into the lake and were drowned.

[14] The men in charge of them took to their heels and carried the news to the town and countryside; and the people came out to see what had happened. [15] When they came to Jesus and saw the madman who had been possessed by the legion of demons, sitting there clothed and in his right mind, they were afraid. [16] When eyewitnesses told them what had happened to the madman and what had become of the pigs, [17] they begged Jesus to leave the district. [18] As he was getting into the boat, the man who had been possessed begged to go with him. [19] But Jesus would not let him. 'Go home to your own people,' he said, 'and tell them what the Lord in his mercy has done for you.' [20] The man went off and made known throughout the Decapolis what Jesus had done for him; and everyone was amazed.

[21] As soon as Jesus had returned by boat to the other shore, a large crowd gathered round him. While he was by the lakeside, [22] there came a synagogue president named Jairus; and when he saw him, he threw himself down at his feet [23] and pleaded with him. 'My little daughter is at death's door,' he said. 'I beg you to come and lay your hands on her so that her life may be saved.' [24] So Jesus went with him, accompanied by a great crowd which pressed round him.

[25] Among them was a woman who had suffered from haemorrhages for twelve years; [26] and in spite of long treatment by many doctors, on which she had spent all she had, she had become worse rather than better. [27] She had heard about Jesus, and came up behind him in the crowd and touched his cloak; [28] for she said, 'If I touch even his

clothes, I shall be healed.' [29] And there and then the flow of blood dried up and she knew in herself that she was cured of her affliction. [30] Aware at once that power had gone out of him, Jesus turned round in the crowd and asked, 'Who touched my clothes?' [31] His disciples said to him, 'You see the crowd pressing round you and yet you ask, "Who touched me?" ' [32] But he kept looking around to see who had done it. [33] Then the woman, trembling with fear because she knew what had happened to her, came and fell at his feet and told him the whole truth. [34] He said to her, 'Daughter, your faith has healed you. Go in peace, free from your affliction.'

[35] While he was still speaking, a message came from the president's house, 'Your daughter has died; why trouble the teacher any more?' [36] But Jesus, overhearing the message as it was delivered, said to the president of the synagogue, 'Do not be afraid; simply have faith.' [37] Then he allowed no one to accompany him except Peter and James and James's brother John. [38] They came to the president's house, where he found a great commotion, with loud crying and wailing. [39] So he went in and said to them, 'Why this crying and commotion? The child is not dead: she is asleep'; [40] and they laughed at him. After turning everyone out, he took the child's father and mother and his own companions into the room where the child was. [41] Taking hold of her hand, he said to her, 'Talitha cum,' which means, 'Get up, my child.' [42] Immediately the girl got up and walked about – she was twelve years old. They were overcome with amazement; [43] but he gave them strict instructions not to let anyone know about it, and told them to give her something to eat.

6 From there he went to his home town accompanied by his disciples. [2] When the sabbath came he began to teach in the synagogue; and the large congregation who heard him asked in amazement, 'Where does he get it from? What is this wisdom he has been given? How does he perform such miracles? [3] Is he not the carpenter, the son of Mary, the brother of James and Joses and Judas and Simon? Are not his sisters here with us?' So they turned against him. [4] Jesus said to them, 'A prophet never lacks honour except in his home town, among his relations and his own family.' [5] And he was unable to do any miracle there, except that he put his hands on a few sick people and healed them; [6] and he was astonished at their want of faith.

Mark now turns from a collection of sayings of Jesus (a feature which is not as frequent in this gospel as in the others) to a series of descriptions of the actions which Jesus performed (a subject which was more congenial to Mark). There are five stories in this section: the storm, the lunatic, the dead girl and the woman, and the visit to the synagogue in Jesus' home town. In telling the stories Mark will emphasize the reactions of the people involved; thus the disciples are called cowards and are said to be afraid with a great fear; people ask Jesus to go away after he has cured the lunatic, and are amazed at what the man says about how he was restored to sanity; the woman has faith, and so does the father of the dead girl; the congregation in the synagogue does not believe, and Jesus is astonished at their unbelief. Mark draws our attention to the various reactions to Jesus, and contrasts the unbelief of some with the faith of the book's audience: they, like the cured lunatic, the woman and the father of the girl, believe him to be the Lord who has power over wind and sea; he will be God's agent for establishing God's rule on the earth; God will put everything under his feet. Jesus gives sanity to those who are mad, holiness to the impure, life to the dead. The audience rejoices in its faith, a miracle and gift that it has received, for which it can claim no credit; and it distances itself from those in the narrative who do not have it: the disciples, the people of the Ten Towns (Decapolis), the mourners in the girl's house and the people in the synagogue.

Mark calls the lake of Gennesaret the sea. It stands for all that is wrong with the world as it is now – especially accidents, disasters and tragedies. When God ruled, there would be no more sea, no more trouble. Jesus would come to bring an end to the present evil age, in which Satan opposed God and afflicted human beings. The unclean spirit in the synagogue at Capernaum had been rebuked with the command, Be muzzled; now the sea is addressed with the same word; Mark's readers will have thought of storms as the effect of personal evil beings that can be controlled by a superior force. Those who are with Jesus in the boat, however, do not believe in him and are greatly afraid and ask who it is that can do this. Faith and fear are opposites, alternatives; if you have faith, you will not be afraid; if you are afraid, it is because you do not believe. But faith is impossible, because it is to say something that is extraordinary and unprecedented; it is to say of one particular human being that he is the final agent of God who will be responsible for the total reconstruction of the universe in such a way that there will be no more disasters, no more chaos. Those who hear or read Mark's book will have complete sympathy with the people in the boat; they will know that their ability to answer the question, Who can this be?, is the result of an action that has been done to them, which they cannot account for entirely. God has given them faith.

The people in the boat said, We are being destroyed! Evil, as Mark has shown us already, is destructive and parasitic; it can only exist by feeding on its host. The lunatic in the next story displays the nature of the demons by his action of gashing himself with stones. The force of his self-destructiveness is such that nobody has been able to control him. Mark and his audience, however, believe that there is no evil that will not be controlled; everything is possible for God. But they also believe that the victory over evil can only come by means of submission to the power of evil; that destruction must run its course, to the very end. The lunatic is restored, but the pigs are destroyed; there is a cost to salvation. When Jesus dies, he will let the evil spirits overwhelm him, and give them his life. This is still in the future from the point of view of the book; all we are allowed to see now is that evil is unremitting in its demands, and will continue to be so, until the final day. This may explain a problem that puzzles us in this story: why is the man, now cured and sane, not allowed to be with Jesus, as he asks? Is it that the reality to which the healing points is not yet complete, and will not be complete, until the Son of Man comes and the angels gather the chosen ones?

The most obvious sign of the fault in the present world-order is death; it is the last enemy, brought upon the world by human beings (they thought) and to be abolished by the new and final

Adam, the saviour and life-giver. Mark helps us to understand the one and only story he has in his book of the resuscitation of a dead person, by repeating a device he had used before: putting another story in the middle of the first. The previous occasion on which he did this was when he inserted the coming of scribes from Jerusalem into the attempt of the family of Jesus to arrest him. Now it is the healing of the woman with the haemorrhages that is put between the beginning and the end of the story of the girl. He draws our attention to the points that are similar; the woman's complaint, for example, had lasted exactly the same length of time as the life of the girl, twelve years. Haemorrhage made you unclean, according to the law, and death removed you from the presence of God: how could you give him thanks from Gehenna? No one had been able to cure the woman, and no one had power to deal with death. The stories are parallel and each illuminates the other. The cure of the woman and the resuscitation of the girl are both signs of what is to happen when evil is overcome and life restored. The woman who believes is not to be afraid, but to go in peace; she is the model for all believers: If I touch even his clothes, I shall be healed. The girl's father is clearly presented with the only two possible alternatives, fear or faith. The parents of the girl are to keep silent about the miracle, because by itself and out of its context in Mark's complete narrative it would mislead those who heard it; the final resurrection, to which this temporary return to life points, will come only after Satan has brought the universe to its total destruction. The impossibility of concealing a girl aged twelve in a first-century Galilean house shows how Mark is not attempting to write a realistic account of what happened; the meaning of the stories is more important to him, and to those for whom he is writing, than the accuracy or practicality of his narrative.

Paul and others had found that Jesus was a stumbling-block when he was preached to Jews, and Mark shows the same response when Jesus attends the synagogue in his home town; he does not name the place, in order that that home town (literally, fatherland) may stand for Judaism as a whole. The congregation in the synagogue recognizes him as the carpenter, the son of Mary and brother of the named male siblings and of the unnamed female siblings. The extent of the list of his relations makes the point that no amount of natural knowledge and factual information will of itself lead to faith. The congregation, we might say, knows everything about Jesus except the one thing that matters; they cannot answer the question that has been asked in the boat, Who can this be? Even Jesus is amazed at this. Usually, in Mark, amazement is the reaction of unbelievers to the words and deeds of Jesus; here, it is the reaction of Jesus to the unbelief of his nation. The only solution is that this is how it always is; God's agents are always rejected by their kindred and compatriots. Faith is not like local patriotism, a natural reaction of support for the lad we all know and have known since he was a child. The more that is known about him as one of us, the less likely we are to believe in him; what matters, in this case, is not his likeness to us, but his difference from us. Faith appreciates and depends on what is distinct. The saviour must be different from those whom he saves.

6.6b–29   The way of death and resurrection

As he went round the villages teaching, [7] he summoned the Twelve and sent them out two by two with authority over unclean spirits. [8] He instructed them to take nothing for the journey except a stick – no bread, no pack, no money in their belts. [9] They might wear sandals, but not a second coat. [10] 'When you enter a house,' he told them, 'stay there until you leave that district. [11] At any place where they will not receive you or listen to you, shake the dust off your feet as you leave, as a solemn warning.' [12] So they set out and proclaimed the need for repentance; [13] they drove out many demons, and anointed many sick people with oil and cured them.

14 Now King Herod heard of Jesus, for his fame had spread, and people were saying, 'John the Baptist has been raised from the dead, and that is why these miraculous powers are at work in him.' 15 Others said, 'It is Elijah.' Others again, 'He is a prophet like one of the prophets of old.' 16 But when Herod heard of it, he said, 'This is John, whom I beheaded, raised from the dead.'

17 It was this Herod who had sent men to arrest John and put him in prison at the instance of his brother Philip's wife, Herodias, whom he had married. 18 John had told him, 'You have no right to take your brother's wife.' 19 Herodias nursed a grudge against John and would willingly have killed him, but she could not, 20 for Herod went in awe of him, knowing him to be a good and holy man; so he gave him his protection. He liked to listen to him, although what he heard left him greatly disturbed.

21 Herodias found her opportunity when Herod on his birthday gave a banquet to his chief officials and commanders and the leading men of Galilee. 22 Her daughter came in and danced, and so delighted Herod and his guests that the king said to the girl, 'Ask me for anything you like and I will give it to you.' 23 He even said on oath: 'Whatever you ask I will give you, up to half my kingdom.' 24 She went out and said to her mother, 'What shall I ask for?' She replied, 'The head of John the Baptist.' 25 The girl hurried straight back to the king with her request: 'I want you to give me, here and now, on a dish, the head of John the Baptist.' 26 The king was greatly distressed, yet because of his oath and his guests he could not bring himself to refuse her. 27 He sent a soldier of the guard with orders to bring John's head; and the soldier went to the prison and beheaded him; 28 then he brought the head on a dish, and gave it to the girl; and she gave it to her mother.

29 When John's disciples heard the news, they came and took his body away and laid it in a tomb.

Mark gives us next the account of the mission of the Twelve, the reaction of Herod to information about Jesus, and the story of the death of the Baptist. Herod thinks that Jesus is John raised from the dead, and that partly explains why Mark gives us at this point in his book the account of John's death, in some detail; he has other reasons also, as we shall see. The story is a flash-back, and it is almost the only part of the book, from the baptism to the burial, when Jesus is not before us on the page.

The Twelve perform exorcisms and healings, and preach the need for repentance; they are not described as proclaiming Jesus as the Lord who will come as the judge of the living and the dead. They cannot preach what they do not yet believe.

The conclusion to which Herod has come, that Jesus is John resurrected, is a near-miss – nearer to the truth than what the Twelve are here saying. Herod is dealing with the central problem, Who can this be? Later, when disciples preach the gospel, they will preach it in terms of one who has been raised from the dead – not John, but Jesus.

The Twelve still need faith to do what they can at this point, before the full meaning of the gospel has been revealed to them. Their faith is demonstrated in the manner of their going, with nothing except a stick. They throw themselves on the mercy of those to whom they preach; and they are to demonstrate the extreme importance of their presence and activity by the gesture of shaking dust from their sandals as a warning sign to those who do not believe: they separate themselves from them completely, so that they will have nothing in common with those who do not believe, when the judgement finally comes – not even the dust of their roads.

The confusion between John the Baptist, Jesus and Elijah, in the minds of some, contrasts with Mark's very precise beliefs and distinctions. He knows the prophecy of Malachi (4.5–6) that God will send Elijah before the day of the Lord; he believes that the Baptist is Elijah, and that Jesus has said so. Moreover he sees in the death of the Baptist a repetition of events in the life of Elijah: King Ahab's queen, Jezebel, had threatened to kill Elijah, but failed (1 Kings 19.1ff.); now Herod, another weak king, is forced by his evil queen, Herodias, to execute John (that is, Elijah). They have at last done to him what they wanted, as the scriptures say of him; and they have succeeded because evil gathers more power as it moves towards its final abolition.

The death of the Baptist gives rise to a (mistaken) faith in his continuing work; This is John, whom I beheaded, raised from the dead. When the gospel is preached and its results are seen, it will be because Jesus, not John, has been raised from the dead.

The faith of the Twelve will be inferior to the faith of the Baptist's disciples: when they hear about the death of their master, they come and take his corpse and lay it in a tomb, whereas Jesus' disciples flee when he is arrested and leave it to someone who is not a disciple to ask for the body of Jesus, be given the corpse, and lay it in a tomb.

6.30–56   Faith and misunderstanding

[30] The apostles rejoined Jesus and reported to him all that they had done and taught. [31] He said to them, 'Come with me, by yourselves, to some remote place and rest a little.' With many coming and going they had no time even to eat. [32] So they set off by boat privately for a remote place. [33] But many saw them leave and recognized them, and people from all the towns hurried round on foot and arrived there first. [34] When he came ashore and saw a large crowd, his heart went out to them, because they were like sheep without a shepherd; and he began to teach them many things. [35] It was already getting late, and his disciples came to him and said, 'This is a remote place and it is already very late; [36] send the people off to the farms and villages round about, to buy themselves something to eat.' [37] 'Give them something to eat yourselves,' he answered. They replied, 'Are we to go and spend two hundred denarii to provide them with food?' [38] 'How many loaves have you?' he asked. 'Go and see.' They found out and told him, 'Five, and two fish.' [39] He ordered them to make the people sit down in groups on the green grass, [40] and they sat down in rows, in companies of fifty and a hundred. [41] Then, taking the five loaves and the two fish, he looked up to heaven, said the blessing, broke the loaves, and gave them to the disciples to distribute. He also divided the two fish among them. [42] They all ate and were satisfied; [43] and

twelve baskets were filled with what was left of the bread and the fish. [44] Those who ate the loaves numbered five thousand men.

[45] As soon as they had finished, he made his disciples embark and cross to Bethsaida ahead of him, while he himself dismissed the crowd. [46] After taking leave of them, he went up the hill to pray. [47] It was now late and the boat was already well out on the water, while he was alone on the land. [48] Somewhere between three and six in the morning, seeing them labouring at the oars against a head wind, he came towards them, walking on the lake. He was going to pass by them; [49] but when they saw him walking on the lake, they thought it was a ghost and cried out; [50] for they all saw him and were terrified. But at once he spoke to them: 'Take heart! It is I; do not be afraid.' [51] Then he climbed into the boat with them, and the wind dropped. At this they were utterly astounded, [52] for they had not understood the incident of the loaves; their minds were closed.

[53] So they completed the crossing and landed at Gennesaret, where they made fast. [54] When they came ashore, he was recognized at once; [55] and the people scoured the whole countryside and brought the sick on their beds to any place where he was reported to be. [56] Wherever he went, to village or town or farm, they laid the sick in the market-place and begged him to let them simply touch the edge of his cloak; and all who touched him were healed.

The key question, Who can this be?, which was raised when Jesus calmed the storm, has still to be answered by the disciples. They do not know who he is, and the signs that he performs do not lead them to faith in him. The disciples in the narrative are in an entirely different position from the readers or hearers of the book who believe that Jesus is God's Son, in whom God delights; he will do the Father's will, and through him God's final and perfect rule over the universe will be effected.

The theme of the central part of Mark's gospel is the contrast between faith and misunderstanding. The signs that Jesus performs should lead to faith on the part of those who are present, but they do not; the characters in the story lack discernment.

There are three parties in the account of the feeding of the five thousand: Jesus, the crowd and the apostles (this is probably the only place in Mark where the word is used, and it could have its non-technical meaning: those who had been sent out). Mark says very little about the crowd, and concentrates our attention on Jesus and the disciples. His intention had been to be alone with them, in order that they might rest; but this was made impossible by the crowd, whose purpose is not expressed immediately, but is probably to be understood as seeking healing for the sick. What is stated, however, is the compassion that Jesus has for them, and that is contrasted with the attitude of the disciples; their only suggestion is that Jesus should dismiss them immediately to go and buy themselves something to eat. Let them care for themselves: we cannot do anything. This highly practical suggestion is rejected by Jesus, who tells the disciples to give them what they have; they do not need more than what is already available. This then turns out to be five loaves and two fish. Jesus blesses God for this gift and the disciples distribute it; and there is so much left over after they have all eaten that it fills twelve baskets. Only then, as a final touch, does Mark tell us the size of the crowd: there were five thousand men (i.e. males; he says nothing about how many women and children there may have been).

At its most accessible level, it is a story of faith in contrast with unbelief: the faith of Jesus, who is prepared to attempt to feed a huge crowd of people with a handful of loaves and a couple of fish; and the absence of faith on the part of the disciples, who can see no further than what is obvious to anybody: that the only thing to do now is to call it a day and send everyone off to fend for themselves. There are other themes that can be found in the story, which was popular in the church; it is the only miracle that is recorded in all four gospels in almost identical words. There is, for example, the well-known Old Testament tradition concerning Moses and the manna in the wilderness; the story of Elisha feeding a hundred men with twenty barley loaves (they ate and had some left over); the expectation that the manna, the bread from heaven, would be eaten again in the age to come; the idea of eating bread as an image of salvation, participation in the feast of the age to come (Give us today the bread of tomorrow); and the symbolism of the eucharist. All or any of these may be there in the story of the feeding, waiting for the alert reader to pick them up; but what Mark invites us to see above all, through the way that he tells the story, is the contrast between the faith of Jesus and the attitude of the disciples, that they can do nothing in the situation, but only leave the crowd to cope on their own. There is nothing in Mark's version of the story that draws our attention to the reaction of the crowd, and this is unusual in Marcan miracles; we expect to be told that the crowd was amazed, or said, Who is this? or, Can this be the prophet? Mark wants us to concentrate on Jesus and the disciples: his compassion and their bewilderment; his ability to deal with the situation and their failure to do so. This may be why the crowd plays such a minor role in the story.

Early in the gospel, after dealing with the crowd, Jesus withdrew to pray (1.35); his real purpose lies in his relationship with the Father, and the Father's with him, not in performing signs with all their ambiguity and the possibility of their being misunderstood. Here again he withdraws to pray; and the disciples, left to themselves, are exposed to a contrary wind and extreme fear; but when Jesus is with them, there is calm. If they had learnt the lesson of the loaves, that God can do anything, they would not have been afraid when they saw Jesus walking on the sea. He was going to pass by them, but he turned aside to them, in order that he might overcome their fear. He said, It is I; and if they had understood who it was who said this, they would not have been afraid. Their fear is the evidence of their unbelief.

The people at Gennesaret recognize him, but only as the miraculous healer; they bring their sick to him, and everyone is healed. Mark tells us this without comment, but by now we should be able to understand what he is saying without further help. The crowd is completely without understanding of the significance of what is happening; what is to be believed is far from everyone's mind.

7.1–23 Commandment and tradition

A group of Pharisees, with some scribes who had come from Jerusalem, met him [2] and noticed that some of his disciples were eating their food with defiled hands – in other words, without washing them. [3] (For Pharisees and Jews in general never eat without washing their hands, in obedience to ancient tradition; [4] and on coming from the market-place they never eat without first washing. And there are many other points on which they maintain traditional rules, for example in the washing of cups and jugs and copper bowls.) [5] These Pharisees and scribes questioned Jesus: 'Why do your disciples not conform to the ancient tradition, but eat their food with defiled hands?' [6] He answered, 'How right Isaiah was when he prophesied about you hypocrites in these words: "This people pays me lip-service, but their heart is far from me: [7] they worship me in vain, for they teach as doctrines the commandments of men." [8] You neglect the commandment of God, in order to maintain the tradition of men.'

[9] He said to them, 'How clever you are at setting aside the commandment of God in order to maintain your tradition! [10] Moses said, "Honour your father and your mother," and again, "Whoever curses his father or mother shall be put to death." [11] But you hold that if someone says to his father or mother, "Anything I have which might have been used for your benefit is Corban," ' (that is, set apart for God) [12] 'he is no longer allowed to do anything for his father or mother. [13] In this way by your tradition, handed down among you, you make God's word null and void. And you do many other things just like that.'

[14] On another occasion he called the people and said to them, 'Listen to me, all of you, and understand this: [15] nothing that goes into a person from outside can defile him; no, it is the things that come out of a person that defile him.'

[17] When he had left the people and gone indoors, his disciples questioned him about the parable. [18] He said to them, 'Are you as dull as the rest? Do you not see that nothing that goes into a person from outside can defile him, [19] because it does not go into the heart but into the stomach, and so goes out into the drain?' By saying this he declared all foods clean. [20] He went on, 'It is what comes out of a person that defiles him. [21] From inside, from the human heart, come evil thoughts, acts of fornication, theft, murder, [22] adultery, greed, and

malice; fraud, indecency, envy, slander, arrogance, and folly; [23] all
these evil things come from within, and they are what defile a person.'

Mark believed that the opposition to Jesus was led by those who
were religious, such as the scribes from Jerusalem, and the
Pharisees. Jerusalem is the only place in the book where a purely
negative and destructive miracle will take place (the cursing of
the fig tree), and that is the only miracle that is performed in
Jerusalem in Mark's account (unlike the other gospels). It will be
religious people who plot Jesus' arrest and death, and religious
people, chief priests and scribes, will be among those who mock
him while he is on the cross.

Mark prepares us for this, now, in the present section of his
book; he explains the reason for the opposition between Jesus
and the religious leaders; they neglect the commandment of God,
he says, in order to maintain the tradition of men. The example
which is then given is the fifth of the ten commandments, Honour
your father and mother, in contrast with the man-made tradition
that this commandment could be avoided if one declared one's
property set aside for God. What Jesus is attacking is the use of
religion for one's own purposes and to further one's own ends
– clearly a perversion of the real aim of the law, which was to
show us how to love God and our neighbour as ourselves.

The occasion that provokes the dispute is to do with hand-
washing, a religious activity, not part of the written law but a
practice observed by Pharisees (and, Mark says, by all the Jews).
To insist on this, as these Pharisees and scribes are doing, is to set
up a tradition and exalt it into a position of such importance that
anyone who does not observe it is condemned and regarded as
out of favour with God.

Mark believes that this is not what is required. Eating, he
believes, has nothing to do with cleanness or holiness before
God; Paul had come to the same conclusion when he wrote his
letter to the Romans. What defiles comes from within, from a
person's thoughts and intentions. The principle is stated in the

39

form of a riddle, that it is not what goes in that defiles, but what comes out; and this is explained to the disciples, who as usual have not understood what the saying means. The implication is that all foods are clean, a conclusion that abrogates much of the Old Testament law.

In the world to which Mark's book belongs, people supposed that they thought with their hearts, not with their heads. The brain was not treated as of any importance; mental activity took place in the heart, which was not understood as a pump for the circulation of the blood until the seventeenth century. To say, therefore, that defilement springs from the thoughts of the heart is to say that what separates us from God is not anything that is physical, but what is mental; not ritual, but moral.

The irony of the situation is that it is those who believe that they are keeping the law and maintaining holiness by opposing Jesus, who are in fact defiling themselves by what they are doing; theirs are the evil thoughts of murder, malice and slander, which lead them to put Jesus to death. Religion can produce some of the worst, as well as some of the best, actions in the world; it is never completely free from ambiguity.

7.24–37   Two signs

[24] He moved on from there into the territory of Tyre. He found a house to stay in, and would have liked to remain unrecognized, but that was impossible. [25] Almost at once a woman whose small daughter was possessed by an unclean spirit heard of him and came and fell at his feet. [26] (The woman was a Gentile, a Phoenician of Syria by nationality.) She begged him to drive the demon out of her daughter. [27] He said to her, 'Let the children be satisfied first; it is not right to take the children's bread and throw it to the dogs.' [28] 'Sir,' she replied, 'even the dogs under the table eat the children's scraps.' [29] He said to her, 'For saying that, go, and you will find the demon has left

your daughter.' ³⁰ And when she returned home, she found the child lying in bed; the demon had left her.

³¹ On his journey back from Tyrian territory he went by way of Sidon to the sea of Galilee, well within the territory of the Decapolis. ³² They brought to him a man who was deaf and had an impediment in his speech, and begged Jesus to lay his hand on him. ³³ He took him aside, away from the crowd; then he put his fingers in the man's ears, and touched his tongue with spittle. ³⁴ Looking up to heaven, he sighed, and said to him, 'Ephphatha,' which means 'Be opened.' ³⁵ With that his hearing was restored, and at the same time the impediment was removed and he spoke clearly. ³⁶ Jesus forbade them to tell anyone; but the more he forbade them, the more they spread it abroad. ³⁷ Their astonishment knew no bounds: 'All that he does, he does well,' they said; 'he even makes the deaf hear and the dumb speak.'

If defilement is moral, not ceremonial, if it is brought about by mental activity, not by eating unclean food, then the distinction between Jew and Gentile becomes questionable. Can holiness be passed down by birth? Are those who have not been initiated into Israel thereby outside the family of God? The paragraph that follows the sayings about clean and unclean describes an incident in which this issue is raised, and it is raised, initially, by Jesus himself in a surprising way, because he speaks as though he maintained the law and its teaching; but then, as the story proceeds, he does not.

The mother of the sick girl is a non-Jew; hers is the only case of a non-Jewish person being involved in a healing in this gospel, where the reader's attention is drawn to the fact. She asks Jesus to drive the demon out of her daughter, and he replies that it is not right to take the food that is meant for the children (that is, for Israel) and throw it to the dogs (the Gentiles). The children must be fed, first: the dogs can be given their dinner later. But the woman takes up his parable and turns it back on him, arguing that this is not how it actually happens; the dogs eat while the children are eating, because they pick up the scraps that the children drop. So, if this is the appropriate analogy, why should she not have what she asks for, immediately? Jesus, we know, believes that anything is possible for faith; he had said so to another woman, earlier in the book (5.34). Faith is a kind of insight into how things really are. This woman clearly has it, too. She goes home and finds that the child is well.

Not only is this the sole case in Mark of the healing of a person explicitly said to be a Gentile, it is also the one instance in this gospel of a miracle performed at a distance. Jesus does not enter the Gentile woman's house; he has no direct contact with the girl; they never see one another. Mark presumably knows that in historical fact Jesus did not have face-to-face dealings with Gentiles, and that the insight that the gospel should be preached to people who were not Jews came later, when the church had pondered the teaching that defilement was entirely ethical and that salvation knew no racial boundaries. The way in which Mark has told the story (always to be observed carefully) preserves the space between Jesus as he was before the crucifixion and the Gentile child; and this points to the historical fact that Jesus dealt only with Jews, and that the question of preaching to Gentiles arose after the resurrection, as both the letters of Paul and the Acts of the Apostles show.

This story is unique in Mark for another reason: it is the only one in which Jesus is presented to us as changing his mind. Here too, and in a bold way, Mark uses a detail in the way he tells the story to refer to the reality to which the story points. There was a change of mind in the churches. Should the gospel be preached to Gentiles before Israel as a whole had heard it? Should the children be fed first? The answer that Paul gave to this question caused a rift with the Jerusalem church and, on one occasion at least, with Peter, as we can see from Paul's letter to the Galatians.

The other sign, which follows immediately, raises once again the question, Who can this be? The man on whom the miracle is performed is a deaf stammerer, and Mark uses a rare Greek word to describe him, so rare, in fact, that it may have been meant to recall in his hearers' memories an Old Testament prophecy.

(Rightly or wrongly, we cannot tell which, Mark assumes throughout his book that those who read it have minds stocked with knowledge of the scriptures of the Jews, in the Greek translation.)

> Then the eyes of the blind will be opened,
> and the ears of the deaf unstopped.
> Then the lame will leap like deer,
> and the tongue of the stammerer speak plainly.
> (Isaiah 35.5–6)

Mark keeps his characters in suspense; they can recognize Jesus as the healer who brings hearing to the deaf and speech to the dumb; but can they see more than this? Above all, can they say what it is that is really happening – that to which these miracles refer: the coming of God's final rule on the earth? And even if they recognized that, there would be something further that they could not possibly know at this point in the narrative, because it has not yet been given to them; namely, how evil will be destroyed and how those who save their lives do it by self-destruction. Jesus forbids the onlookers to say anything, because what they would say would have to be inadequate; they say it, nevertheless, and it is inadequate. They can only describe the healings, not what these healings signify. They are, in fact, in the same situation as the man who was healed: they are deaf, and they speak with difficulty. What was done to him must be done to them, but at a more significant level.

8.1–26   Jesus bestows insight

There was another occasion about this time when a huge crowd had collected, and, as they had no food, Jesus called his disciples and said to them, [2] 'My heart goes out to these people; they have been with me now for three days and have nothing to eat. [3] If I send them home hungry, they will faint on the way, and some of them have a long way to go.' [4] His disciples answered, 'How can anyone provide these people with bread in this remote place?' [5] 'How many loaves have you?' he asked; and they answered, 'Seven.' [6] So he ordered the people to sit down on the ground; then he took the seven loaves, and after giving thanks to God he broke the bread and gave it to his disciples to distribute; and they distributed it to the people. [7] They had also a few small fish, which he blessed and ordered them to distribute. [8] They ate and were satisfied, and seven baskets were filled with what was left over. [9] The people numbered about four thousand. Then he dismissed them, [10] and at once got into the boat with his disciples and went to the district of Dalmanutha.

[11] Then the Pharisees came out and began to argue with him. To test him they asked him for a sign from heaven. [12] He sighed deeply and said, 'Why does this generation ask for a sign? Truly I tell you: no sign shall be given to this generation.' [13] With that he left them, re-embarked, and made for the other shore.

[14] Now they had forgotten to take bread with them, and had only one loaf in the boat. [15] He began to warn them: 'Beware,' he said, 'be on your guard against the leaven of the Pharisees and the leaven of Herod.' [16] So they began to talk among themselves about having no bread. [17] Knowing this, he said to them, 'Why are you talking about having no bread? Have you no inkling yet? Do you still not understand? Are your minds closed? [18] You have eyes: can you not see? You have ears: can you not hear? Have you forgotten? [19] When I broke the five loaves among five thousand, how many basketfuls of pieces did you pick up?' 'Twelve,' they said. [20] 'And how many when I broke the seven loaves among four thousand?' 'Seven,' they answered. [21] He said to them, 'Do you still not understand?'

[22] They arrived at Bethsaida. There the people brought a blind man to Jesus and begged him to touch him. [23] He took the blind man by the hand and led him out of the village. Then he spat on his eyes, laid his hands upon him, and asked whether he could see anything. [24] The man's sight began to come back, and he said, 'I see people – they look like trees, but they are walking about.' [25] Jesus laid his hands on his eyes again; he looked hard, and now he was cured and could see everything clearly. [26] Then Jesus sent him home, saying, 'Do not even go into the village.'

Mark will now repeat the sequence he has just completed: a feeding miracle, crossing the lake, controversy with Pharisees, rebuke of disciples and restoration of faculties. This time round, however, the sequence will lead into a passage in which we shall be told who Jesus is, what he must do, and how his disciples are to follow him.

Though the sequence of events here is similar to what came before, there are differences, and they are significant. The crowd who are fed this time are described in a different way from the previous crowd: there they were said to be like sheep without a shepherd (an expression used frequently of Israel in the Old Testament) but these have come from far, a description of the Gentiles (e.g. Isaiah 57.19; see Ephesians 2.17); the numbers in the two stories are different, and they may point to the same idea, a Jewish crowd first, and a Gentile crowd second (four thousand, seven loaves and seven baskets; compare four corners of the earth, and the idea that there were seventy nations in the world). If this were Mark's meaning, it would chime in with his belief that Jesus was the saviour of all, Gentile or Jew.

The disciples are again presented in the way that we saw them before; they have learnt nothing from the former feeding miracle; they still express incredulity and have nothing positive to offer: How can anyone provide these people with bread in this remote place? The attitude of Jesus is still the same, compassion for the crowd; and so is his instruction to the disciples, to find out what there is to hand. Coming so soon after the story of the Gentile woman and her statement about the bread that the dogs eat (Jews called Gentiles 'dogs') we can see the appropriateness of this second feeding story at this point in the book: Jesus is the one who gives his life for everybody.

The Pharisees tempt Jesus to perform a miracle to authenticate himself (a sign from heaven means an act of God), and in this they reveal the blindness that is inevitable among those who do not believe. Faith is one way of seeing things; not the only way, and not a way that anyone is compelled to take. Mark intends the feeding stories (and all the miracles) to be read as signs from heaven; so, to ask for one immediately after one has been given is to declare one's blindness to what has been already provided. Those who ask for signs in this context should not be given more; they would not recognize them if they were granted.

The disciples are as blind and deaf and dumb and forgetful as the Pharisees. They do not use their minds. They have been given fourteen miracles that Mark has described in detail, and there will be four more in the book. But they still worry about bread, when they have one loaf with them in the boat.

Once more the numbers are rehearsed, to underline the enormity of the disciples' failure: five loaves for five thousand, and twelve baskets over; seven loaves for four thousand and seven baskets over. The figures may or may not be significant in themselves, and we may or may not be able to recover Mark's meaning; but at least we can see this: in each case there was more left over at the end than there had been at the beginning; and in between, thousands of people had been fed. Therefore there is no need for the disciples to be worried that they have no bread. One loaf is enough. What they should take note of is the leaven of the Pharisees and the leaven of Herod.

The only other place in Mark where Pharisees and Herod (or rather, Herod's party) are mentioned together is at the end of the series of conflict stories, when they took counsel to destroy Jesus (3.6). Since then, we have seen Herod's destruction of the Baptist. The disciples are to beware of the religious and political leaders: they will bring about Jesus' death and that of his followers.

In the previous sequence, Jesus healed a man who stammered and people expressed a half-formed faith: All he does, he does well. At least they did not say that he acted through the power of Beelzebul, as the Jerusalem scribes had done. In this second sequence, the person who is healed is blind; and in both cases, the cure involves the use of Jesus' spittle. The description of this healing, however, is unlike that of all the other healings in the book, in that it happens in two stages: first, the man sees people, but they look to him like trees, except that they walk; in the second stage of the healing, everything is clear. We cannot be certain, but it is at least a possibility that Mark describes the healing of the blind man in this particular way, in order to compare it with the paragraph that he will put next in his book. The question will be, Who do people say that I am? Some will say one thing, some another, and neither will be the whole truth. The question will be put again, this time to the disciples, and Peter will say, You are the Messiah. Faith is seeing, but seeing more clearly than those who do not have it; and to have it is a miracle, as anyone who has ever believed anything knows. It is something received and understood.

The man who was blind is told not to tell anyone in the village about his cure (according to what seems to have been the original text of Mark; see REB margin), because it is not his cure that is important; what matters is the significance of the cure, its use as a figure of the gift of faith and of faith's effect.

------------------◆------------------

8.27 – 9.1 New teaching

27 Jesus and his disciples set out for the villages of Caesarea Philippi, and on the way he asked his disciples, 'Who do people say I am?' 28 They answered, 'Some say John the Baptist, others Elijah, others one of the prophets.' 29 'And you,' he asked, 'who do you say I am?' Peter replied: 'You are the Messiah.' 30 Then he gave them strict orders not to tell anyone about him; 31 and he began to teach them that the Son of Man had to endure great suffering, and to be rejected by the elders, chief priests, and scribes; to be put to death, and to rise again three days afterwards. 32 He spoke about it plainly. At this Peter took hold of him and began to rebuke him. 33 But Jesus, turning and looking at his disciples, rebuked Peter. 'Out of my sight, Satan!' he said. 'You think as men think, not as God thinks.'

34 Then he called the people to him, as well as his disciples, and said to them, 'Anyone who wants to be a follower of mine must renounce self; he must take up his cross and follow me. 35 Whoever wants to

> save his life will lose it, but whoever loses his life for my sake and for the gospel's will save it. [36] What does anyone gain by winning the whole world at the cost of his life? [37] What can he give to buy his life back? [38] If anyone is ashamed of me and my words in this wicked and godless age, the Son of Man will be ashamed of him, when he comes in the glory of his Father with the holy angels.'
>
> 9 He said to them, 'Truly I tell you: there are some of those standing here who will not taste death before they have seen the kingdom of God come with power.'

Mark is now approximately half-way through his book, and it is here, at the middle of it, that he introduces new themes and abandons old ones. There will, for example, be less frequent accounts of miracles performed by Jesus, from now until the end of the book. There have been fifteen so far, but only three will follow: a possessed boy, a blind man, and the destruction of a fig tree; and in each case there will be features of the miracle that make it appropriate to its position in the latter part of the book.

But the change in the character of the story that Mark is telling goes further than the comparative absence of miracles. Jesus had said earlier that nothing was hidden except to be disclosed, and nothing concealed except to be brought into the open (4.22), and it is this revealing of something previously hidden that now takes place, and dominates the second half of the book, determining the choice of its contents.

For some pages before this point the reader has observed the characters in the narrative puzzling over the problem, Who can this be? Jesus will now put the question to Peter, and Peter will reply; but his answer will be only half the truth, and Mark immediately makes it obvious that Peter has not understood what he has said. He is like the man who saw people as trees walking. He has used the term 'the Messiah' (in Greek, 'the Christ'), an expression that Mark thinks appropriate to Jesus; he had used it in the first line of the book, The beginning of the gospel of Jesus Christ, and he will put it into the mouth of Jesus later in the narrative (9.41, 13.21; cf.14.61–62). Paul had used it as if it were no more than another name; he spoke of Jesus, or Christ, or Jesus Christ, or Christ Jesus, without implying any difference of meaning. Mark, however, regards The Christ as the title of an office; but there is very little evidence that Jews had used it in this way before the time of Jesus or of Paul. Mark seems to be unaware of this, and puts it into the mouth of the high priest as though it were a commonplace expression: Are you the Messiah? (14.61). Mark's understanding, then, is that the Jews looked forward to the coming of a deliverer whom they spoke of as the Messiah; and this became the traditional teaching among Christians, until it was challenged in the present century.

To some extent, therefore, the question that has been hanging over the heads of the characters has now been answered: Who can this be? He is the Messiah. But that is not the whole answer; Mark is too profound a thinker to suppose that anything is dealt with satisfactorily by simply giving it a name. Writing, even writing a gospel, is no substitute for reality. What the Messiah will have to do, when the moment comes, will be so over-whelming that even the one who bears the title will be shattered by it.

Again and again, in the first half of the book, we saw how when Jesus performed a miracle, he frequently accompanied it by a command to silence; and how, when demons and unclean spirits said who he was, he made them keep quiet. The reason for this was in order that the reader should not think that salvation lay merely in deliverance from one power by the action of one who was stronger; the method is not miracles. Therefore the account of them was qualified by the command not to speak about them. Now, however, in the second half of the book, there are, as we saw, far fewer miracles; and they do not attract commands to silence (9.27; 10.52; 11.20ff.). But, instead, it is the use of the title Messiah that is to be kept secret: he gave them strict orders not to tell anyone about him (8.30).

The reason why they are not to use the title is given in the next sentence, and it is this that sets the tone for the rest of the book: He began to teach them that the Son of Man had to endure great suffering, to be rejected by the elders, chief priests, and scribes; to be put to death, and to rise again three days afterwards. This is the first clear, explicit and detailed statement of what is to happen in the remaining narrative; it will be repeated in more or less the same words as Jesus and his disciples go from Galilee to Jerusalem, and it will occupy the final pages of the book as the narrative slows down to its final stopping-point. Everything that is in the book will be there in order to illuminate this prediction: this is the one and only way for the Son of Man to go, and it is the only way for his followers, too. Jesus speaks about it plainly. The lamp that is not brought to be put under a measuring bowl or under a bed (4.21) is the good news of a rejected Messiah.

Peter acts on behalf of everybody; he took hold of Jesus and began to rebuke him. (It is the same word that was used when Jesus rebuked the demons and unclean spirits.) Destruction cannot be the way. Right up to the end of the book (or even after, as far as the reader of the book knows) Peter never gets beyond this. His faith, if he has any, is not described by Mark, and he is not used as a model for other followers. The women will be commanded to tell his disciples and Peter, but they will say nothing to anyone. The faith, or the unbelief, of others does nothing to ease the question, Do you believe?

Peter is rebuked (the same word) and is dismissed from the presence of Jesus for thinking human thoughts. An unaccepted Messiah is a stumbling-block to everybody; it is the good news that nobody wants to hear.

The six verses that follow (8.34 – 9.1) are closely interconnected; they follow one another in a logical sequence that is developed out of the first prediction of the death and resurrection of the Son of Man. Everybody who wants to be a follower of his must travel the way he goes; they must embrace destruction. They must stop working for their own good, and making that the motive for their existence. To renounce self means to disown one's self, to dissociate one's self from the claims that the self makes. It is the same word that will be used of Peter saying that he does not know Jesus. In the end, these are the only alternatives that we have: to disown yourself, or to disown Christ. Peter will choose the second; the follower of Jesus must choose the first. (The teaching that is being given here assumes that human beings have this extraordinary ability to transcend themselves, and distinguish between the I that observes and the me that is observed. There will be no let-up in the conflict between these two.)

The followers of Jesus are to take up their cross; they are to co-operate with their own execution. Cross, here, at its first occurrence in the book, should not be trivialized. It refers to capital punishment of slaves in the Roman Empire, and at various periods and places it was a common enough sight. It is unlikely that it had become a metaphor for mere discomfort or voluntary self-deprivation by this time, any more than the electric chair or the gas chamber has with us. The followers must follow: Mark says it, because everybody will do anything to avoid it, as Peter has already demonstrated, even before Jesus had said it.

The underlying principle is then stated with brutal clarity: attempting to save your life is in fact self-destruction, but self-destruction is salvation. Not all self-destruction; only when it is for the sake of Jesus and for the sake of the gospel. There could be a self-destruction that was entirely evil, as we were shown in the case of the man with the legion of demons and as we shall see again in the boy who has the dumb and deaf spirit. The extraordinary offensiveness of this teaching is concealed through the usual translation of the verb as 'lose': whoever loses his life, etc. But there are well-established word-pairs, both in Greek and in English; one is 'save' and 'destroy', the other is 'find' and 'lose'. The pair that is used here should be 'save' and 'destroy'. God can be described as the one who is able to save life or to destroy it (James 4.12), and the context in Mark requires the contrast between two kinds of deliberate action: it is hard to see how anyone can be commanded to lose something; losing is normally involuntary. To take up your cross is to do something.

As we shall see when Mark describes the approach to death of the one whom the disciples must follow, there will be nothing to suggest that the belief that self-destruction is the only way annuls or even reduces the horror at what is to happen (14.33). The prediction of rising again after three days does not take away the terror of death, nor is the promise of resurrection held out as a reward to encourage the followers to die. The requirement of death and the promise of resurrection stand side by side, neither diminishing the other. Death must be total giving, as though there were nothing to come after; and resurrection must be the completely gratuitous action of God, concerning which we may not presume.

The next step in the argument is the statement that one's life is irreplaceable. There would be no sense in which one could own the world, if one were not there to be the possessor of it. There is only one way of having everything, and that must include having your life also. But this is not an option; what is required is the destruction of your life, for Christ's sake and the gospel's. Nothing is more valuable than your life; there is nothing you can exchange it for, because if you give it away, you will not be there to receive whatever it is that you are swopping it for. It is this life, the *sine qua non* for having anything, the irreplaceable and infinitely valuable state of existing, that must be destroyed, and the followers of Jesus are given the command to do so.

This teaching was objectionable, because it required those who heard it to abandon everything that resisted shame, in a society where shame was to be avoided almost more than anything else. Crucifixion involved nakedness, lack of self-respect, any sense of well-being or of having made a success of one's life and opportunities. (Mark will portray all this, in detail, when the time is ripe.) To be ashamed of Jesus would be to separate oneself from him and to reject what he is saying. But it would be more than that: it would be to separate oneself from those who really are his followers. (See REB margin, 'me and mine': this is probably what Mark wrote; his way of using possessive pronouns shows it.) They have been left with no sense of well-being, or self-respect, or success. Any withdrawal from them and any surrender due to shame will be endorsed by the Son of Man when he comes in glory to judge the world, to send the angels to collect the chosen into the kingdom and to dismiss the wicked into Gehenna. To separate oneself from Christ's shame, before he comes in glory, would be to destroy oneself in the wrong way: those who want to save their lives will only make an end of them.

This future event, when the Son of Man would return, Mark believed, was coming soon. There must be judgement and sorting out, before the time when God would rule. His whole book is written under the heading, The kingdom of God is coming soon. If that is so, then the separation of those who will enter from those who will not, must also be coming soon; so soon, Mark believed, that some of those living at the time of Jesus would see it happen while they were still alive.

Mark wrote his book, using the ideas and expressions that were available to him at that time and in that place, whenever and wherever it was. He could not have written this book without those ideas and that tradition. His sources were Jewish apocalyptic, the preaching of John the Baptist and of Jesus, and the teaching of Paul. All of them expected the present world-order to end soon; and it did not happen as they had thought. If it had happened, we should not be here, and the world would not have continued as it was before, with sickness, sin, lunacy, disasters and death. It was, if we may put it like this, a concession to our weakness that the society in which Jesus lived and called his disciples to follow him, was a society in which the imminent end of the present order was generally expected. We do not take seriously what will not affect us personally.

9.2–29 Jesus and his way

[2] Six days later Jesus took Peter, James, and John with him and led them up a high mountain by themselves. And in their presence he was transfigured; [3] his clothes became dazzling white, with a whiteness no bleacher on earth could equal. [4] They saw Elijah appear and Moses with him, talking with Jesus. [5] Then Peter spoke: 'Rabbi,' he said, 'it is good that we are here! Shall we make three shelters, one for you, one for Moses, and one for Elijah?' [6] For he did not know what to say; they were so terrified. [7] Then a cloud appeared, casting its shadow over them, and out of the cloud came a voice: 'This is my beloved Son; listen to him.' [8] And suddenly, when they looked around, only Jesus was with them; there was no longer anyone else to be seen.

[9] On their way down the mountain, he instructed them not to tell anyone what they had seen until the Son of Man had risen from the dead. [10] They seized upon those words, and discussed among themselves what this 'rising from the dead' could mean. [11] And they put a question to him: 'Why do the scribes say that Elijah must come first?' [12] He replied, 'Elijah does come first to set everything right. How is it, then, that the scriptures say of the Son of Man that he is to endure great suffering and be treated with contempt? [13] However, I tell you, Elijah has already come and they have done to him what they wanted, as the scriptures say of him.'

[14] When they came back to the disciples they saw a large crowd surrounding them and scribes arguing with them. [15] As soon as they saw Jesus the whole crowd were overcome with awe and ran forward to welcome him. [16] He asked them, 'What is this argument about?' [17] A man in the crowd spoke up: 'Teacher, I brought my son for you to cure. He is possessed by a spirit that makes him dumb. [18] Whenever it attacks him, it flings him to the ground, and he foams at the mouth, grinds his teeth, and goes rigid. I asked your disciples to drive it out, but they could not.' [19] Jesus answered: 'What an unbelieving generation! How long shall I be with you? How long must I endure you? Bring him to me.' [20] So they brought the boy to him; and as soon as the spirit saw him it threw the boy into convulsions, and he fell on the ground and rolled about foaming at the mouth. [21] Jesus asked his father, 'How long has he been like this?' 'From childhood,' he replied; [22] 'it has often tried to destroy him by throwing him into the fire or into water. But if it is at all possible for you, take pity on us and

help us.' ²³ 'If it is possible!' said Jesus. 'Everything is possible to one who believes.' ²⁴ At once the boy's father cried: 'I believe; help my unbelief.' ²⁵ When Jesus saw that the crowd was closing in on them, he spoke sternly to the unclean spirit. 'Deaf and dumb spirit,' he said, 'I command you, come out of him and never go back!' ²⁶ It shrieked aloud and threw the boy into repeated convulsions, and then came out, leaving him looking like a corpse; in fact, many said, 'He is dead.' ²⁷ But Jesus took hold of his hand and raised him to his feet, and he stood up.

²⁸ Then Jesus went indoors, and his disciples asked him privately, 'Why could we not drive it out?' ²⁹ He said, 'This kind cannot be driven out except by prayer.'

The prediction that the kingdom of God would come with power before some of those who were alive at the time of Jesus had died, leads straight into the next paragraph; Mark describes how Jesus is disclosed to three of his disciples as he will be seen when he comes in the glory of his Father at the end of this age to judge the living and the dead. The whiteness of his clothes shows that he belongs to God and comes from heaven, as it will again in the case of the young man at the tomb, at the end of the book (16.5). Elijah and Moses were both believed to have been taken up alive into heaven (though this would be no longer relevant in the case of Elijah, if, as Mark believed, he had returned as John the Baptist and been beheaded). The key to understanding the passage as a whole may lie in Peter's suggestion: Shall we make three shelters, one for you, one for Moses, and one for Elijah? Mark's comment that Peter did not know what to say, and that all three disciples were terrified, indicates that Peter's proposal is a mistake. The detailed elaborateness of the question – as though two of them might have shared one shelter, and the third might have been kept vacant for any other visitors from heaven – draws our attention to its complete inappropriateness; Peter, as so often in Mark, has said what he should not have said. His mistake lies in the actual details of the proposal: he has put Jesus as one of three, alongside Elijah and Moses; each is to have his own shelter. The voice from heaven corrects Peter's mistake and distinguishes Jesus from the rest of mankind; he is the one and only Son of God. God had spoken of him through Moses when he had said, To him you shall listen (Deuteronomy 18.15). The disciples are to attend to Jesus, not to Elijah or to Moses; what Jesus will say will be different from what was said in the past. (We have seen this already in the declaration that food does not create uncleanness; we shall hear it again when the issue of divorce is raised; and the experimental proof of God's existence by a miracle, which Elijah had set up, will be subverted when Jesus dies.) The story ends with the disappearance of Elijah and Moses, and the continuing presence of Jesus only; that is how it is to be, from now on. He is to be their one teacher, pattern, and guide, and all that was given before in the law and the prophets is to be seen only as leading to him, having no independent status or authority. Not only this, but he and he alone can be their saviour, because only he can do what is required.

Mark's gospel, unlike the other three (which were written later), has no account of appearances of Jesus after the resurrection; the original text of Mark ended where some of the oldest manuscripts still end, with the silence of the women at the tomb (16.8; it is now thought that anything printed in a Bible after this was added by later scribes). When the young man in the white garment tells the women that Jesus is risen and that his disciples will see him in Galilee, that will be the time to make public the vision that Peter, James and John had of the Lord who will come in glory. Hence the instruction to the disciples not to tell anyone what they had seen until the Son of Man had risen from the dead. When therefore the readers of Mark reach the final paragraph of the book, and are told that Jesus is risen (16.6), the description that Mark has given here in the Transfiguration, with its divine authentication of Jesus as the one to whom they are to listen, will immediately spring to mind. Henceforth they will be waiting for him to return, keeping hold of the command that Jesus had given them, Stay awake (13.37). Instead of resurrection appearances (to others in the past), Mark puts before his readers the pre-view of the coming of the Son of Man to which they are to look forward. What matters to Mark is not that there was faith among the original disciples (he leaves us uncertain whether there was), but that there should be faith among those who hear and read his book.

There had, apparently, been no expectation in pre-Christian Judaism that individuals would rise from the dead at different points in time (even though Mark attributed such an idea to Herod and others: 6.14ff.). What was expected was the general resurrection of all the dead together on the same day, and even that was not believed by Sadducees. The disciples' difficulty, what this rising from the dead of the Son of Man could mean, draws the readers' attention to the subject. (This is a device Mark uses more than once: characters in the narrative are said to have problems that readers of the book will also have.) Mark may not describe the Easter appearances, but he has no doubt about the truth of the resurrection; he refers to it again and again. Notice, for example, that each of the three predictions of the passion is also a prediction of the resurrection.

In Malachi (4.5–6), as also in Ecclesiasticus (48.10), it had been said that Elijah would return, and reconcile parents to their children and children to their parents, lest God should come and put the earth under a ban to destroy it. The disciples ask Jesus about this, attributing it to the scribes. Jesus agrees, but says that the scriptures state that the Son of Man is to suffer and to be treated with contempt. (The particular passages that Mark will have had in mind will become apparent when he writes his account of the passion.) What Elijah does, therefore, does not exclude the ill-treatment of the Son of Man who comes after him. Evil and destruction will have their way with the Son of Man as they have already had it with Elijah (that is, John the Baptist): Jezebel's intention has been fulfilled by Herodias. The scriptures therefore are not to be interpreted in such a way as to make the suffering of Jesus (or of his followers) unnecessary: rather, the suffering of Jesus is to be taken as the key to the understanding of the scriptures. This insistence on the inevitability of destruction, death and resurrection will now be illustrated in the final exorcism in the gospel, which follows immediately.

The rest of the disciples are discovered arguing with scribes (a word that links this paragraph to the one before) and surrounded by a crowd. The crowd, Mark says, was overcome with awe at the arrival of Jesus and ran to greet him: he does not say why. Is it, perhaps, that the problem that faces the disciples and the scribes can only be solved when Jesus returns to them?

The father of a sick son explains that there is a spirit in the boy that makes him dumb and brings on spasms. The disciples had not been able to cast it out. Jesus calls them unbelievers, and says that he finds them unendurable. When the boy is brought to Jesus, the spirit demonstrates its destructiveness, which has been how it was for the boy since childhood: trying to destroy him in fire and water. The father asks for the compassion of Jesus, if it is possible; and Jesus replies, Everything is possible to the one who believes. The father declares that he has faith and unbelief. Jesus commands the spirit to come out, and again it reveals its destructive power before it does so. It leaves the boy apparently dead, but Jesus raises him up.

Of all the exorcisms (or indeed of any healing miracles that Mark records), this is the fullest, with the greatest number of details. He has kept it for this part of his book, because it illustrates the theme he is pursuing here, that the way to salvation is through destruction. He repeats the words for emphasis: the boy became as if he were dead; many said he had died; Jesus raised him up and he arose. The followers of Jesus must die and be raised to life, must share destruction and salvation. The possessed boy is the model for all believers.

The failure of the disciples to perform the exorcism is explained as failure to pray. Jesus, who prays in the evening (6.46) and at midnight (14.35) and in the early morning (1.35), is renewed and empowered when it is dark: prayer is entry into darkness and silence, from which healing comes. The disciples have failed to do this, and that was why they could not drive the spirit out.

The section that ends here has borne out what had been said earlier (8.27ff.): Jesus is not Elijah, nor is he one of the prophets; he is the one, unique Son of God who is different from everybody else because he will come as their judge at the end of this age. Meanwhile, he is to be rejected, treated with contempt and put to death. This is the way by which evil will be overcome. Satan and his agents depend for their existence on destroying: let them, then, destroy Jesus and his followers, and indeed the whole universe that God has made. God is the God who raises the dead; the healing of the possessed boy symbolizes the way of salvation: destruction first, then resurrection. But the disciples remain without understanding; they cannot heal, because they do not pray. Prayer is a kind of dying and rising, participation both in the darkness and in the light.

9.30–50 How to destroy yourself

[30] They left that district and made their way through Galilee. Jesus did not want anyone to know, [31] because he was teaching his disciples, and telling them, 'The Son of Man is now to be handed over into the power of men, and they will kill him; and three days after being killed he will rise again.' [32] But they did not understand what he said, and were afraid to ask.

[33] So they came to Capernaum; and when he had gone indoors, he asked them, 'What were you arguing about on the way?' [34] They were silent, because on the way they had been discussing which of them was the greatest. [35] So he sat down, called the Twelve, and said to them, 'If anyone wants to be first, he must make himself last of all and servant of all.' [36] Then he took a child, set him in front of them, and put his arm round him. [37] 'Whoever receives a child like this in my name,' he said, 'receives me; and whoever receives me, receives not me but the One who sent me.'

[38] John said to him, 'Teacher, we saw someone driving out demons in your name, and as he was not one of us, we tried to stop

him.' [39] Jesus said, 'Do not stop him, for no one who performs a miracle in my name will be able the next moment to speak evil of me. [40] He who is not against us is on our side. [41] Truly I tell you: whoever gives you a cup of water to drink because you are followers of the Messiah will certainly not go unrewarded.

[42] 'If anyone causes the downfall of one of these little ones who believe, it would be better for him to be thrown into the sea with a millstone round his neck. [43] If your hand causes your downfall, cut it off; it is better for you to enter into life maimed than to keep both hands and go to hell, to the unquenchable fire. [45] If your foot causes your downfall, cut it off; it is better to enter into life crippled than to keep both your feet and be thrown into hell. [47] And if your eye causes your downfall, tear it out; it is better to enter into the kingdom of God with one eye than to keep both eyes and be thrown into hell, [48] where the devouring worm never dies and the fire is never quenched.

[49] 'Everyone will be salted with fire.

[50] 'Salt is good; but if the salt loses its saltness, how will you season it? 'You must have salt within yourselves, and be at peace with one another.'

The second prediction of the death and resurrection of the Son of Man acts as the text which is then expounded in the stories and sayings that follow it. The teaching is for the disciples alone, but they do not understand it or receive it; they are afraid to ask, and where there is fear, there is no faith. They have not yet realized what the connection is between suffering and God's will, or how destruction and salvation are related to each other in the divine plan.

This second prediction is the shortest of the three, and it concentrates on the necessity of dispossessing oneself; the Son of Man must be handed over to people who will destroy him: this will be the means by which the world will be saved. Jesus must will his death; God will raise him up. The reaction of the disciples is entirely understandable; Jesus himself will be horrified by the event, when it finally draws near (14.33).

With only a very few exceptions, the disciples have been presented as people who failed to understand, ever since the parable of the sower had had to be explained to them (chapter 4); they will continue in this way until they leave the narrative: the main group at the moment when Jesus is arrested, and Peter when he is condemned to death. Their failure now and all along is their inability to follow Jesus in the way that he is going; they discuss who is the greatest, and this shows that they are still far from realizing the implications of the new teaching. The saying, If anyone wants to be first, he must make himself last of all and servant of all, must not be taken as if it were a prescription for promotion to higher office. Being last in the line and the waiter at the meal ('servant' here means one who brings the food to the table) is the end to be pursued, without any thought of it being a means to something else. Ambition is not sanctified by being turned into the desire to be first in the age to come.

The significance of the child is not to do with some aspect of the character that is supposed to be present in children, such as meekness, gratitude, openness to new ideas, trustfulness and so on. Children were not thought of in this way in the ancient world (or in any other age, before the nineteenth century). The meaning of the action of taking a child lies in the fact that children were regarded as non-persons: they could not own property; they had no status in law, no rights; babies could be, and were, exposed in order that they might die. Paul had expressed the attitude of his time to children when he had said, They are no different from slaves (Galatians 4.1); you could not get much lower than that. To be like a child meant to be without experience, lacking the wisdom that comes with age; a mouth to feed rather than a pair of hands to contribute to the family's welfare. Childhood was a negative condition, to be grown out of as quickly as possible. It would be disastrous for a nation if children were its rulers (Isaiah 3.4). Therefore when Jesus takes a child, and makes it a symbol of himself, he is declaring himself the one who is the last and the least, the servant of all. And yet he is the representative of God, the One who sent me. God gives himself in what seems the least godly way; not in majesty and power, but in a naked man on the foreigners' cross. The only way to receive him will be by sharing

61

his humiliation, shame and contempt. This is the diametric opposite of wanting to be first.

John (the brother of James, 1.19) speaks twice in Mark – here, and in the next chapter. On both occasions he is in the wrong. Here, he is in favour of excluding non-members from an activity that he thinks should be restricted to members only. Jesus has no time for this kind of zeal; he will not allow his disciples to become a closed shop. If the exorcist uses his name, and if it is successful, he will not speak evil of Jesus. Such people should be given the benefit of the doubt, and the disciples should be biased in their favour.

To be a disciple of the Messiah is to belong to him, and any good thing that is done to a disciple will be rewarded by God. (This is the only instance of the word 'reward' in Mark's gospel, whereas Matthew has it ten times. Mark is far more aware of the dangers of covetousness than his successor; in Mark, the only place where a reward is mentioned is here in a promise made to those who do not belong to the Messiah, but perform the least kindness to those who do.)

The implication of this is seen by considering the opposite case: evil done to disciples (little ones) will be punished in the coming judgement. Anything that leads to sin is to be forcefully removed. The rule that salvation comes through destruction applies here as elsewhere: cut out whatever tempts you; a restricted life is better than a full life, if the full life is to end in destruction in Gehenna.

The two ways of leaving the place of the last judgement are called, on the one hand, 'life' (verses 43 and 45) or 'the kingdom of God' (verse 47), and, on the other hand, Gehenna, the unquenchable fire. Disowning one's self, destroying one's life, cutting out what causes sin – this is the only way to live; the other is the way to miss life and cease to exist.

The saying, Everyone will be salted with fire, is a parody of an instruction in Leviticus (2.13), Every sacrifice is to be salted with salt. (Some scribes, copying Mark, inserted the quotation from Leviticus, because they saw the connection.) Under the old covenant, sacrifices were made acceptable to God by the addition of salt; but now the worshippers offer themselves as their sacrifice; and what makes them acceptable to God is not salt, but fire: that is, destruction. This is the salt of the new covenant, and it is essential and irreplaceable. Without it, there can be no peace in the community of the followers of the Messiah. Discussing which is greatest can only lead to divisions and bitterness; *memento mori*, remembering your destruction, is the shortest route to fellowship.

10.1–31   Entry into the kingdom of God

On leaving there he came into the regions of Judaea and Transjordan. Once again crowds gathered round him, and he taught them as was his practice. [2] He was asked: 'Is it lawful for a man to divorce his wife?' This question was put to test him. [3] He responded by asking, 'What did Moses command you?' [4] They answered, 'Moses permitted a man to divorce his wife by a certificate of dismissal.' [5] Jesus said to them, 'It was because of your stubbornness that he made this rule for you. [6] But in the beginning, at the creation, "God made them male and female." [7] "That is why a man leaves his father and mother, and is united to his wife, [8] and the two become one flesh." It follows that they are no longer two individuals: they are one flesh. [9] Therefore what God has joined together, man must not separate.'

[10] When they were indoors again, the disciples questioned him about this. [11] He said to them, 'Whoever divorces his wife and remarries commits adultery against her; [12] so too, if she divorces her husband and remarries, she commits adultery.'

[13] They brought children for him to touch. The disciples rebuked them, [14] but when Jesus saw it he was indignant, and said to them, 'Let the children come to me; do not try to stop them; for the kingdom of God belongs to such as these. [15] Truly I tell you: whoever does not accept the kingdom of God like a child will never enter it.' [16] And he put his arms round them, laid his hands on them, and blessed them.

[17] As he was starting out on a journey, a stranger ran up, and, kneeling before him, asked, 'Good Teacher, what must I do to win eternal life?' [18] Jesus said to him, 'Why do you call me good? No one is good except God alone. [19] You know the commandments: "Do not murder; do not commit adultery; do not steal; do not give false evidence; do not defraud; honour your father and mother." ' [20] 'But Teacher,' he replied, 'I have kept all these since I was a boy.' [21] As Jesus looked at him, his heart warmed to him. 'One thing you lack,' he said. 'Go, sell everything you have, and give to the poor, and you will have treasure in heaven; then come and follow me.' [22] At these words his face fell and he went away with a heavy heart; for he was a man of great wealth.

[23] Jesus looked round at his disciples and said to them, 'How hard it will be for the wealthy to enter the kingdom of God!' [24] They were amazed that he should say this, but Jesus insisted, 'Children, how hard it is to enter the kingdom of God! [25] It is easier for a camel to pass through the eye of a needle than for a rich man to enter the kingdom of God.' [26] They were more astonished than ever, and said to one another, 'Then who can be saved?' [27] Jesus looked at them and said, 'For men it is impossible, but not for God; everything is possible for God.'

[28] 'What about us?' said Peter. 'We have left everything to follow you.' [29] Jesus said, 'Truly I tell you: there is no one who has given up home, brothers or sisters, mother, father or children, or land, for my sake and for the gospel, [30] who will not receive in this age a hundred times as much – houses, brothers and sisters, mothers and children, and land – and persecutions besides; and in the age to come eternal life. [31] But many who are first will be last, and the last first.'

The section begins with a reference to the journey that Jesus and the disciples are making, from Capernaum (mentioned at 9.33) to Judaea and Transjordan. Jerusalem, where the journey will end, will not be mentioned until 10.32, but we know already that this is where the final events will take place; in the first prediction of the death and resurrection we were told that he would be rejected by the elders and the chief priests and the scribes, and this could only happen in Jerusalem.

The first paragraph in this section might seem misplaced. All the other incidents, from Peter's declaration at Caesarea Philippi to the arrival at Jerusalem, are related in some way to the theme that the disciples must follow Jesus to enter the kingdom of God; but in this paragraph (verses 1–12) the subject is remarriage after divorce, which sounds more like detailed ethical teaching than the subjects that dominate Mark's book: the coming judgement and the way to live in view of it. It may be, however, that Mark saw the passage in a different way. The question about divorce is answered with the counter-question, What did Moses command you? Moses permitted it (Deuteronomy 24.1ff.); but, Jesus says, this was because the Israelites were unteachable, their minds could not grasp what God willed for them. What that was could be seen from other texts, earlier in the law (namely Genesis 1.27 and 2.24), that described the creation of male and female at the beginning of the world, and how a man leaves his parents to be united with his wife. (We had a similar example of setting texts against one another in 9.11ff.) What had been the case in the beginning is to be so again in the age to come; there will be no place for stubbornness then. Moreover, leaving parents for a new life with one's spouse is a parable of discipleship, and the command that man must not separate what God has joined together can be read as a promise that God will not allow anything to break the fellowship between Jesus and the disciples. God has taken the disciples from their families and united them with Jesus; he will not go back on what he has done. Read in this way, the paragraph is highly relevant to the context in which Mark has put it. (See Ephesians 5.25–33 for similar use of Genesis 2.24.)

The story about the children, brought for Jesus to touch, that is, to bless, comes next, and once more the disciples are seen to be in the wrong; children are those who will enter the kingdom when it comes, because they represent all those who are unimportant (in their own opinion) and have no skill or status or possessions. Here, as before in chapter 9 (verse 36), Jesus hugs children; they are the only people in Mark that he does hug. He thereby declares that entry into the kingdom will be for those whose only title to it is that they have no title to it.

The third element in this section, and the longest, is the story of the rich man; it follows on immediately from the story of the children, and it makes the same point, that what is required is to have nothing: this is how it is with children; this is not how it is with the rich. The man asks what he must do to gain possession of eternal life (which has already been used as a synonym for the kingdom of God, see 9.43, 45, 47). Jesus rebukes him for calling him 'good'; that should be applied only to God; Jesus is not moved by flattery – a dishonest attempt to persuade somebody to act in your interest. He quotes from the commandments, and what we have heard already in the book has prepared us for what follows. The man says he has kept the commandments since he was a boy. (He is not a rich young man in Mark; he is no longer young. It is Matthew who calls him a young man: 19.20.) Before we hear the reply of Jesus, Mark inserts a comment that is surprising and unexpected: Jesus looked at him and loved him. (There is no need for the translation in the REB, 'His heart warmed to him'.) This rich man, who employs flattery and believes he has kept the whole of the law since childhood, is the only person in Mark of whom it is said that Jesus loved him. And that is not all. He will not become a disciple, but will go away sad. The only 'disciple whom Jesus loved' in Mark is the person who could not accept the demands that Jesus made of him; he saw what was involved and he went away. Others thought that they could do what was required (Peter, James, John) and could not; this man knew that he could not and accepted it. One suspects that Mark thought that the latter showed greater insight than the former. There is nothing to be done with self-confidence except to destroy it.

The man was very rich; he had everything except the one thing he needed – poverty. To say, You lack one thing, to a rich man, who can buy anything he wants, is a joke, because what he inevitably lacks is not having anything. He cannot be like the children, unless he gets rid of what he has. The only way to possess everything is by having nothing.

The disciples are surprised that it will be hard for the rich to enter the kingdom; it had often been said in the scriptures that God showed his approval of the righteous by giving them prosperity. The Psalmist had never seen a righteous man begging. What is being said here is the opposite: that wealth is a curse, not a blessing. It is hard for anyone, rich or poor, to enter the kingdom, but it is impossible for the rich, as impossible as it would be to pass a real live camel through the eye of an ordinary sewing needle – i.e. the largest commonly seen animal through the smallest opening. This leads the disciples to greater astonishment: Who can be saved? means Who can enter the kingdom?

Mark has one further unexpected and astonishing insight. Everything is possible for God, even the saving of the rich. Jesus loves the person who knows that he cannot cope with what is expected; he will act on their behalf, as Mark will soon tell us; he will die for them.

Finally, Peter asks about those who are disciples and believe themselves to be owed something from God. Jesus agrees: those who have given things up for the sake of Jesus and the gospel (cf. 8.35) will be repaid; but with persecutions, in this age; and in the age to come, with eternal life. Yet neither Peter nor the readers of Mark should think that they are in a position to put a bill in to God for repayment. God is not in debt to us, and we cannot calculate what we are owed by him. He is in sole command, and he decides how he will deal with us. Our idea of priority is not his; and our idea of what is shameful is not his. The last judgement will involve the overturning of our expectations.

10.32–52 The road to Jerusalem

³² They were on the road going up to Jerusalem, and Jesus was leading the way; and the disciples were filled with awe, while those who followed behind were afraid. Once again he took the Twelve aside and began to tell them what was to happen to him. ³³ 'We are now going up to Jerusalem,' he said, 'and the Son of Man will be handed over to the chief priests and the scribes; they will condemn him to death and hand him over to the Gentiles. ³⁴ He will be mocked and spat upon, and flogged and killed; and three days afterwards, he will rise again.'

³⁵ James and John, the sons of Zebedee, approached him and said, 'Teacher, we should like you to do us a favour.' ³⁶ 'What is it you want me to do for you?' he asked. ³⁷ They answered, 'Allow us to sit with you in your glory, one at your right hand and the other at your left.' ³⁸ Jesus said to them, 'You do not understand what you are asking. Can you drink the cup that I drink, or be baptized with the baptism I am baptized with?' ³⁹ 'We can,' they answered. Jesus said, 'The cup that I drink you shall drink, and the baptism I am baptized with shall be your baptism; ⁴⁰ but to sit on my right or on my left is not for me to grant; that honour is for those to whom it has already been assigned.'

⁴¹ When the other ten heard this, they were indignant with James and John. ⁴² Jesus called them to him and said, 'You know that among the Gentiles the recognized rulers lord it over their subjects, and the great make their authority felt. ⁴³ It shall not be so with you; among you, whoever wants to be great must be your servant, ⁴⁴ and whoever wants to be first must be the slave of all. ⁴⁵ For the Son of Man did not come to be served but to serve, and to give his life as a ransom for many.'

⁴⁶ They came to Jericho; and as he was leaving the town, with his disciples and a large crowd, Bartimaeus (that is, son of Timaeus), a blind beggar, was seated at the roadside. ⁴⁷ Hearing that it was Jesus of Nazareth, he began to shout, 'Son of David, Jesus, have pity on me!' ⁴⁸ Many of the people told him to hold his tongue; but he shouted all the more, 'Son of David, have pity on me.' ⁴⁹ Jesus stopped and said, 'Call him'; so they called the blind man: 'Take heart,' they said. 'Get up; he is calling you.' ⁵⁰ At that he threw off his cloak, jumped to his feet, and came to Jesus. ⁵¹ Jesus said to him, 'What do you want me to do for you?' 'Rabbi,' the blind man answered, 'I want

my sight back.' [52] Jesus said to him, 'Go; your faith has healed you.'
And at once he recovered his sight and followed him on the road.

This group of passages begins and ends with a reference to the road by which Jesus and the disciples were travelling to Jerusalem, and along which the man who had been blind will follow them. The Greek word that is used is the one that is also translated as 'the Way', a title used sometimes for the followers of Jesus before the word 'Christianity' was coined in the early second century. In the literal sense, the group led by Jesus is moving towards the city that the Jews regard as the focal point of their history and religion; but in a metaphorical sense, Mark is teaching his readers the new way to live that Jesus has taught and demonstrated. The disciples are still incapable of understanding what they are being told; they are separated from Jesus by fear. (There is no justification for the REB's translation 'awe'; Mark always means by this word a reaction that is inappropriate, the result of unbelief; 'awe' is a word that can be used in a context that implies approval, but Mark did not approve of the Twelve.)

The section opens with the third and final prediction of death and resurrection; it is also the most detailed of the three, emphasizing the humiliation of the Son of Man, who will be mocked, spat upon, flogged and killed by the Gentiles. It will take more than words to persuade the disciples to believe this; only the event when it happens will make any difference to them. This will not be described in Mark's book; the purpose of the book is to create faith in those who hear it and read it. We are not allowed to think of faith as occurring in other people, lest that should diminish the force of its impact on us.

Mark has already established the pattern whereby immediately after a prediction of the Son of Man's death and resurrection the disciples demonstrate their inability to comprehend what is said to them; he repeats the sequence here, with the story of the request of James and John. They want the best seats at the coming banquet; they see the age to come as a time of splendour for Jesus and his followers, and they suppose that glory can be allocated in advance. Not even Jesus can promise personal favours to his followers; to think of the future in the way that James and John are doing is to misunderstand how it is related to the present. We have no recipe for glory; there is nothing we can do to guarantee that we shall receive it. All we have is the way of destruction: the cup that Jesus will drink is his death; the baptism with which he will be baptized is his inundation in total isolation from disciples, family and God. What is needed is complete undoing, so that not even the promise of glory will be left; if it were, then the stripping would not be complete. Jesus and his followers have no assurances about the future, other than the bare hope; hope that could be visualized would not be hope. To wait in hope is to wait without knowing what it is you are waiting for. Mark will tell us that the Son knows neither the day nor the hour when the end will come (13.32); neither can he arrange the seating for the feast.

Mark had warned us, only a few pages earlier, that to be at peace with one another we must have salt within ourselves; and that this salt is fire, destruction, and its acceptance (9.49–50). What happens next illustrates the teaching given there: the ten disciples are indignant with James and John because of their ambition for glory. They are all still mesmerized by the question, Who is the greatest? (9.34) and, like Peter, they think as men think, not as God thinks (8.33). In the world, rulers keep their positions by displaying power and suppressing revolutions with force. But that is not how it is with the disciples. (Mark almost certainly wrote 'is' here, not 'shall be' as in the manuscripts which the REB has followed. Jesus points to how it is between the disciples and himself, at that time; not to some future relationship in the church, after the resurrection.) The way it is with the disciples is that wanting glory must be abandoned, and replaced by being the waiter and the slave for the others in the group. This is how Jesus relates to them; he is the one who waits on them, and he will do this supremely in his death: it will be for many, that is, for everybody else (one plus many equals all); it will release them from their imprisonment in misunderstanding, sin and disintegration.

Once this has been said, the solution to the problem that has been with us at least since Caesarea Philippi is revealed. What is needed is someone to do something for the disciples who are blind, deaf, dumb, paralysed, fainting with hunger. Jesus is the waiter, as he is also the healer; what he brings is his life, given over to death on behalf of those who cannot do anything for themselves.

Mark had assured us that everything was possible for God, but the intractability of the disciples had strained our belief that they could ever be reformed. Now, however, Mark begins to show us how the story will turn out. The passion and resurrection of Jesus will make it possible for the disciples to follow him, because he will undergo death for them, in their absence. Paul had explained this to the Christians in Rome: it was while we were helpless, sinners, enemies, that Christ died for us and thus reconciled us to God (Romans 5.6ff.).

The cure of the blind beggar is the last healing miracle in the book, and it is placed here because it expresses exactly what Mark wants to say at this point. Jesus can have followers; real followers, not people like the disciples and Peter. Or, if that is to put it too harshly, Jesus can make even people like the disciples and Peter into real followers. All that is needed is the request of the beggar, Have pity on me (in Greek, *eleēson me*). He has faith in Jesus as Son of David; he knows what he needs: sight. He receives what he asks for, and demonstrates the cure by following Jesus on the road (or 'in the way' or even 'in the Way'), to Jerusalem, to death and resurrection, and to the kingdom of God.

11.1–25   Jesus arrives in Jerusalem

They were now approaching Jerusalem, and when they reached Bethphage and Bethany, close by the mount of Olives, he sent off two of his disciples. [2] 'Go into the village opposite,' he told them, 'and just as you enter you will find tethered there a colt which no one has yet ridden. Untie it and bring it here. [3] If anyone asks why you are doing this, say, "The Master needs it, and will send it back here without delay." ' [4] So they went off, and found the colt outside in the street, tethered beside a door. As they were untying it, [5] some of the by-standers asked, 'What are you doing, untying that colt?' [6] They answered as Jesus had told them, and were then allowed to take it. [7] So they brought the colt to Jesus, and when they had spread their cloaks on it he mounted it. [8] Many people carpeted the road with their cloaks, while others spread greenery which they had cut in the fields; [9] and those in front and those behind shouted, 'Hosanna! Blessed is he who comes in the name of the Lord! [10] Blessed is the kingdom of our father David which is coming! Hosanna in the heavens!'

[11] He entered Jerusalem and went into the temple. He looked round at everything; then, as it was already late, he went out to Bethany with the Twelve.

[12] On the following day, as they left Bethany, he felt hungry, [13] and, noticing in the distance a fig tree in leaf, he went to see if he could find anything on it. But when he reached it he found nothing but leaves; for it was not the season for figs. [14] He said to the tree, 'May no one ever again eat fruit from you!' And his disciples were listening.

[15] So they came to Jerusalem, and he went into the temple and began to drive out those who bought and sold there. He upset the tables of the money-changers and the seats of the dealers in pigeons; [16] and he would not allow anyone to carry goods through the temple court. [17] Then he began to teach them, and said, 'Does not scripture say, "My house shall be called a house of prayer for all nations"? But you have made it a robbers' cave.' [18] The chief priests and the scribes heard of this and looked for a way to bring about his death; for they were afraid of him, because the whole crowd was spellbound by his teaching. [19] And when evening came they went out of the city.

[20] Early next morning, as they passed by, they saw that the fig tree had withered from the roots up; [21] and Peter, recalling what had happened,

said to him, 'Rabbi, look, the fig tree which you cursed has withered.' [22] Jesus answered them, 'Have faith in God. [23] Truly I tell you: if anyone says to this mountain, "Be lifted from your place and hurled into the sea," and has no inward doubts, but believes that what he says will happen, it will be done for him. [24] I tell you, then, whatever you ask for in prayer, believe that you have received it and it will be yours.

[25] 'And when you stand praying, if you have a grievance against anyone, forgive him, so that your Father in heaven may forgive you the wrongs you have done.'

In the world of the Hebrew scriptures, ability to predict future events accurately was evidence of divine inspiration. Samuel, for example, had told Saul whom he would meet when he left the town where Samuel had anointed him (1 Samuel 10); when it happens exactly as he has said, we know that the events are the work of God. Mark has two examples of this device: here, at the entry of Jesus into Jerusalem; and on the day before the Passover, when disciples are sent to prepare for the evening meal.

Riding into Jerusalem on a colt on which no one had previously ridden is an enacted fulfilment of an Old Testament prophecy:

> Daughter of Zion, rejoice with all your heart,
> shout in triumph, daughter of Jerusalem!
> See, your king is coming to you,
> his cause won, his victory gained,
> humble and mounted on a donkey,
> on a colt, the foal of a donkey.
>
> (Zechariah 9.9)

In the Greek translation, which is the version Mark and his readers seem to have known best, the colt is described as 'new', which matches what Jesus says: A colt which no one has yet ridden. For spreading clothes for a king to walk on, compare 2 Kings 9.13. Bartimaeus' faith had been that Jesus was the Son of David, the king whom God had promised long ago; and now the crowd greets him, as the one who will establish the final Davidic rule. Hosanna is their prayer, that God in the heavens will save them from the present evil age, and begin his rule.

The whole description of the entry into Jerusalem is steeped in irony. Mark certainly believes that what is about to happen is God's will, that a great event is about to take place in this city through the arrival of Jesus. But he does not speak of it himself in the terms that the crowd uses, nor does he (unlike Matthew) take David as the ideal king of whom Jesus is the expected son. At the beginning of the book, Mark contrasted the intention of Jesus with the expectations of the crowd (1.35ff.); here he has made a similar distinction: the crowd is hoping for a leader who will exercise power, but what will happen will be the total abnegation of control: the Son of Man will be handed over to Gentiles, to be mocked and killed.

Mark then places side by side two accounts, one of Jesus in the temple, and the other of his dealings with a fig tree. The latter is intended to illuminate the former: the tree has the appearance of fruit, but on inspection has only leaves; the temple gives the impression that it is there for the worship of God, but in fact it is a robbers' cave. (Mark signals the symbolic meaning of the fig tree, by reminding us that, if it is the time shortly before Passover, it will not be the season of figs. He has not written a narrative that can be read as a straightforward account of what happened; he has written stories that make sense only when they are referred to the good news of the kingdom.) What will happen to the temple will be like what happens to the fig tree: Not one stone will be left upon another; they will all be thrown down.

The cursing of the fig tree is the last miracle performed by Jesus in Mark's book, and the only one of the miracles that takes place in Jerusalem. We have seen how they decrease in frequency as the book moves towards Jerusalem: when we arrive there, no signs of health, sanity, restoration are given; rather, what we have is the symbol of an ending: May no one ever again eat fruit from you! It is the only entirely destructive miracle of Jesus in Mark's book.

What will take the place of Jerusalem, the temple on mount Zion and the old covenant will be faith in God, and prayer; instead of the one nation, Israel, the new covenant will be for all nations. This mountain on which the temple stands will no longer have the significance it had in the past; faith will remove it into the sea; the new covenant will supersede the old.

REB omits verse 26 from the main text and prints it as a footnote: But if you do not forgive others, then the wrongs you have done will not be forgiven by your Father in heaven. This verse is not in some of the oldest Greek manuscripts and other versions, and may have come in through memory of Matthew 6.15.

11.27 – 12.12   The authority of Jesus

[27] They came once more to Jerusalem. And as he was walking in the temple court the chief priests, scribes, and elders came to him [28] and said, 'By what authority are you acting like this? Who gave you authority to act in this way?' [29] Jesus said to them, 'I also have a question for you, and if you give me an answer, I will tell you by what authority I act. [30] The baptism of John: was it from God, or from men? Answer me.' [31] This set them arguing among themselves: 'What shall we say? If we say, "From God," he will say, "Then why did you not believe him?" [32] Shall we say, "From men"?' – but they were afraid of the people, for all held that John was in fact a prophet. [33] So they answered, 'We do not know.' And Jesus said to them, 'Then I will not tell you either by what authority I act.'

12 He went on to speak to them in parables: 'A man planted a vineyard and put a wall round it, hewed out a winepress, and built a watch-tower; then he let it out to vine-growers and went abroad. [2] When the season came, he sent a servant to the tenants to collect from them his share of the produce. [3] But they seized him, thrashed him, and sent him away empty-handed. [4] Again, he sent them another servant, whom they beat about the head and treated outrageously, [5] and then

another, whom they killed. He sent many others and they thrashed some and killed the rest. [6] He had now no one left to send except his beloved son, and in the end he sent him. "They will respect my son," he said; [7] but the tenants said to one another, "This is the heir; come on, let us kill him, and the inheritance will be ours." [8] So they seized him and killed him, and flung his body out of the vineyard. [9] What will the owner of the vineyard do? He will come and put the tenants to death and give the vineyard to others.

[10] 'Have you never read this text: "The stone which the builders rejected has become the main corner-stone. [11] This is the Lord's doing, and it is wonderful in our eyes"?'

[12] They saw that the parable was aimed at them and wanted to arrest him; but they were afraid of the people, so they left him alone and went away.

The leaders of the Jews in Jerusalem recognize Jesus as a threat; he has created a disturbance in the temple, which is the heart and centre of Judaism. Anyone in the position of the chief priests, scribes and elders would inevitably ask, What is this man's authority for acting in this way? (Questions about authority are much loved by those who think they have it; other people are not so concerned.) It is a notoriously difficult question to answer; one could appeal to scripture, or to a recognized teacher, or, as in the case of the prophets in the Old Testament, to the word of God spoken directly to the prophet: Thus saith the Lord. The difficulty of claiming to speak in the name of God is that it is extraordinarily hard to prove it. The only test offered in scripture was whether what the prophet said came true; but that needed time.

Jesus adopts a method of arguing used by the rabbis; he refuses to answer their question, until they have answered a counter-question, concerning the authority of John the Baptist. Mark's readers believe that both John and Jesus are from God; they have authority from God to do what they do. Both of them are prophets (Jesus spoke of himself as such, 6.4). Both were in conflict with people in authority and died at their hands. Both fulfilled the promises of God made in scripture.

The counter-question of Jesus places the authorities in a dilemma: they cannot say that John was not a prophet, because of the crowd; they cannot say that he was, because they did not believe him. (Presumably they were not baptized, in spite of what is said at 1.5, and they did not believe in the one for whom John had prepared the way.) They refuse to answer, and thus relieve Jesus of any need to answer their question concerning his authority.

The parable that follows, however, contains a further statement of the authority of Jesus. It recalls Isaiah's song of the vineyard (5.1ff.), but with a significant difference: in Isaiah there is no explicit reference to the people of Israel; they are completely concealed in the metaphor of the song; they are the vines that have borne wild grapes. In Mark, on the other hand, the people of Israel are the tenants of the vineyard, and it is their conduct in refusing to deliver up the fruit and in ill-treating those whom the owner sends that is central to the story. No explanation is given as to why the tenants treated the servants with such extraordinary violence; and none is needed, because it was a well-established belief among the Jews at this time that all the prophets had been persecuted.

Mark's irony shows at the point where the owner of the vineyard sends his only son (the same expression that was used at the baptism of Jesus and the transfiguration) and says, They will respect my son. We know that they will not. (Luke, who did not approve of this sort of subtlety, inserts a word to save the appearances – for God: Perhaps they will respect him [20.13]. It is the only instance of this word for 'perhaps' in the New Testament.)

The problem that religious people have to deal with – and it particularly affects those who see themselves as guardians of a tradition – is to distinguish between the honour of God and their own personal investment in it. The parable of the vineyard throws light on this situation. The purpose of the tenants in killing the son is that they may own the property themselves, as they would, if there were no other heir. What those who are supposed to represent God and his interests end up doing is attempting to replace God with themselves. The ultimate lie that evil persuades us to believe is that we are God.

In reality, this is not at all how it is; God will act against those who believe in themselves; the one whom they have rejected will be exalted by God: Jesus will save his life by destroying it. The gospel will be preached to Gentiles, and they will become the tenants of the vineyard.

If the authority of a prophet is to be seen in the fulfilment of his predictions, then Jesus has answered the question concerning the source of his authority. He has prophesied what will happen to him; as soon as the occasion is suitable, it will take place exactly as he has said.

12.13–34   Three questions put to Jesus

[13] A number of Pharisees and men of Herod's party were sent to trap him with a question. [14] They came and said, 'Teacher, we know you are a sincere man and court no one's favour, whoever he may be; you teach in all sincerity the way of life that God requires. Are we or are we not permitted to pay taxes to the Roman emperor? [15] Shall we pay or not?' He saw through their duplicity, and said, 'Why are you trying to catch me out? Fetch me a silver piece, and let me look at it.' [16] They brought one, and he asked them, 'Whose head is this, and whose inscription?' 'Caesar's,' they replied. [17] Then Jesus said, 'Pay Caesar what belongs to Caesar, and God what belongs to God.' His reply left them completely taken aback.

[18] Next Sadducees, who maintain that there is no resurrection, came to him and asked: [19] 'Teacher, Moses laid it down for us that if there are brothers, and one dies leaving a wife but no child, then the next should marry the widow and provide an heir for his brother. [20] Now there were seven brothers. The first took a wife and died without issue. [21] Then the second married her, and he too died without issue; so did the third; [22] none of the seven left any issue. Finally the woman

died. [23] At the resurrection, when they rise from the dead, whose wife will she be, since all seven had married her?' [24] Jesus said to them, 'How far you are from the truth! You know neither the scriptures nor the power of God. [25] When they rise from the dead, men and women do not marry; they are like angels in heaven.

[26] 'As for the resurrection of the dead, have you not read in the book of Moses, in the story of the burning bush, how God spoke to him and said, "I am the God of Abraham, the God of Isaac, the God of Jacob"? [27] He is not God of the dead but of the living. You are very far from the truth.'

[28] Then one of the scribes, who had been listening to these discussions and had observed how well Jesus answered, came forward and asked him, 'Which is the first of all the commandments?' [29] He answered, 'The first is, "Hear, O Israel: the Lord our God is the one Lord, [30] and you must love the Lord your God with all your heart, with all your soul, with all your mind, and with all your strength." [31] The second is this: "You must love your neighbour as yourself." No other commandment is greater than these.' [32] The scribe said to him, 'Well said, Teacher. You are right in saying that God is one and beside him there is no other. [33] And to love him with all your heart, all your understanding, and all your strength, and to love your neighbour as yourself – that means far more than any whole-offerings and sacrifices.' [34] When Jesus saw how thoughtfully he answered, he said to him, 'You are not far from the kingdom of God.' After that nobody dared put any more questions to him.

Questions now come from three groups within Judaism: first, from the Pharisees and supporters of Herod, whom we last saw when they were plotting the destruction of Jesus (3.6, but cf. also 8.15) and that is still their intention; secondly, from the Sadducees, the associates of the priests in the temple; and thirdly, from one of the scribes, who stands apart from the other two groups in that he will be praised for his understanding.

Mark's intention seems to have been to build up a picture of the opposition to Jesus from the various groups that made up first-century Judaism. He wants his readers to see that the message of Jesus brought him into conflict with some of his contemporaries, though not with all (hence the scribe); and that following Jesus would involve breaking away from the temple and the synagogue. Though Mark knows that it was the Romans who were responsible for the crucifixion, he also believes (almost certainly mistakenly) and wants to demonstrate that the authorities of Judaism approved of Jesus' execution and initiated it.

But, as so often in Mark, there seems to be more than one reason for his choice of procedure. Each of the three answers that Jesus gives to these questions contains teaching that will help the reader of the book to make sense of its message: God stands over against us with demands that we cannot pay; he raises the dead, therefore death is not the termination of life; the first commandment is to love God and the second to love your neighbour, compared with which the temple sacrifices are of little importance. What Jesus will do, as the book comes towards its conclusion, will be the one act of obedience to God, the one occasion on which God will be loved with the whole of somebody's heart and understanding and strength; God, in turn, will raise him up to life, because he is the God of the living; and he will accept his life as a ransom for many, paying God what God is owed.

The Pharisees, who approach Jesus with flattery (cf. the rich man: 10.17), say that he teaches correctly the way that God has commanded us to live. (Mark is picking up the expression from 10.52.) Their repeated double question, Are we or are we not to give? Shall we or shall we not give? contrasts with the word that Jesus uses: they are to repay, to give back. They have no choice, so there is no problem. You must pay taxes to the emperor, and you must see yourselves as owing God what he requires of you. The parable of the vineyard had set before us the idea that God is the owner, and his people are tenants who are liable for rent.

It would be a perversion of a religion to think that its pursuit exempted one from obligations to the state or, even worse, to God. It is, however, an easy mistake to make: my zeal for God enables me to see myself as justifiably attracting free benefits from Caesar and from God. Jesus does indeed teach the way of

God in truth, and those who flatter him are hoisted with their own blandishments.

Belief in the restoration of all the dead to life at the end of this age and as a preliminary to the judgement and the age to come, entered Judaism only in the last centuries before Christ (e.g. in Daniel, written *c.* 165 BC). The Sadducees, being conservatives and not welcoming new ideas, did not believe in resurrection; the question about the woman and her seven husbands is intended to show that Moses could not have believed in it, either; for if he had, he would not have laid down a law concerning the marriage of the deceased brother's wife (Deuteronomy 25.5). Like the Pharisees, the Sadducees do not know the truth: resurrection, Jesus says, is both scriptural and possible with God; with regard to its possibility, God has the power to raise the dead to eternal life, when there will be no need for marriage or for further offspring (because there will be no more death); with regard to scripture, the passage in Exodus (3.6) speaks of God declaring himself the God of people who had died but would live, through resurrection. This is the God of Jesus, too; though Jesus will be put to death, he will return as the Son of Man to judge everybody.

The scribe's question was one that was often discussed among the rabbis: Which laws have more weight than others? Is there one commandment that is fundamental to all the rest? The idea that it was the command to love was not unknown in pre-Christian Judaism. (Notice how in Luke the lawyer gives it as the summary of the law, 10.25ff.) What the scribe says, that love is more than whole-offerings and sacrifices, could be taken to mean that it replaces the purpose for which the temple had been built – a place to offer animal sacrifices. (Matthew re-writes Mark here, to preserve the authority of the law: Everything in the law and the prophets hangs on these two commandments, 22.40.)

The death of Jesus will do what the animal sacrifices aimed at, and more. He will make all further sacrifice unnecessary. To see this, as the scribe has done, is to be near to the kingdom of God and to be ready to enter it when it comes.

The three questions were intended to embarrass Jesus and provide a case against him when he was brought to court. They hoped he could be accused of forbidding the payment of taxes, or of teaching what was not in scripture, or of not understanding the law. But instead of embarrassing him, it is they who are embarrassed by his answers; and the reader sees the way with greater clarity.

12.35–44   Three examples of the teaching of Jesus

³⁵ As he taught in the temple, Jesus went on to say, 'How can the scribes maintain that the Messiah is a son of David? ³⁶ It was David himself who said, when inspired by the Holy Spirit, "The Lord said to my Lord, 'Sit at my right hand until I put your enemies under your feet.' " ³⁷ David himself calls him "Lord"; how can he be David's son?'

There was a large crowd listening eagerly. ³⁸ As he taught them, he said, 'Beware of the scribes, who love to walk up and down in long robes and be greeted respectfully in the street, ³⁹ to have the chief seats in synagogues and places of honour at feasts. ⁴⁰ Those who eat up the property of widows, while for appearance' sake they say long prayers, will receive a sentence all the more severe.'

⁴¹ As he was sitting opposite the temple treasury, he watched the people dropping their money into the chest. Many rich people were putting in large amounts. ⁴² Presently there came a poor widow who dropped in two tiny coins, together worth a penny. ⁴³ He called his disciples to him and said, 'Truly I tell you: this poor widow has given more than all those giving to the treasury; ⁴⁴ for the others who have given had more than enough, but she, with less than enough, has given all that she had to live on.'

The three incidents that follow are linked by the repetition of words; in the previous paragraph, a question was asked by a scribe, and now Jesus asks a question about their teaching; he then criticizes scribes, mentioning their treatment of widows; that provides the link with the third element in the section, the praise of a widow who excels in generosity.

In Psalm 110 David (the speaker of the Psalms, as was supposed) refers to the future Messiah who is to sit at God's right hand as 'my Lord'. But the scribes say that the Messiah is a son of David. How can one person be both son and Lord? The answer may perhaps be, By resurrection. After his death, God will say to Jesus, Sit at my right hand; God will raise him and exalt him. David prophesies both the resurrection of Jesus, and his future coming when God will put his enemies under his feet. (Paul had used the same verse from this psalm when writing to the Corinthians about the coming end of this age: see 1 Corinthians 15.20–28.)

The warning against scribes accuses them of being acquisitive, of seeking praise and respect, and even of usurping the property of widows, who were the most vulnerable class in the society of that time. At the coming judgement, they will be condemned for their hypocrisy. They are examples of religion displacing morality; they excuse themselves from the most obvious social obligations on the ground of their duty to God. But the two commandments, to love God and to love your neighbour, stand side by side, and neither can absorb the other, or render it void.

The widow with only two coins that make a penny has three possible courses of action: to give nothing to the temple (and in her case, that would be excusable), to give one coin (which would be generous, because it would be half her total assets), or to give both (which would be unwise, rash, imprudent). She does the third, and Mark underlines the magnitude of what she does by the way he describes it: everything, all that she had, the whole of her existence. The widow has understood what the scribes did not understand, and done what they failed to do: God requires everything; he is to be loved with all that one has. She does this, and it is not Mark's purpose to tell us more than that. He does not explain how she lived afterwards, or who supported her, or what effect it had on them. The book that Mark is writing is not a treatise on holy living, but a gospel; and a gospel deals in extremes and absolutes. God demands all, and gives all; that is the theme, and Mark repeats it as often as he can.

Looking back over these pages of Mark's book, we see that he began them with the saying of Jesus that to destroy one's life for his sake and the gospel's was to save it (8.35); the widow has certainly done that; Jesus will do it, too.

13.1–37 Keep awake

As he was leaving the temple, one of his disciples exclaimed, 'Look, Teacher, what huge stones! What fine buildings!' ² Jesus said to him, 'You see these great buildings? Not one stone will be left upon another; they will all be thrown down.'

³ As he sat on the mount of Olives opposite the temple he was questioned privately by Peter, James, John, and Andrew. ⁴ 'Tell us,' they said, 'when will this happen? What will be the sign that all these things are about to be fulfilled?'

⁵ Jesus began: 'Be on your guard; let no one mislead you. ⁶ Many will come claiming my name, and saying, "I am he"; and many will be misled by them. ⁷ When you hear of wars and rumours of wars, do not be alarmed. Such things are bound to happen; but the end is still to come. ⁸ For nation will go to war against nation, kingdom against kingdom; there will be earthquakes in many places; there will be famines. These are the first birth-pangs of the new age.

⁹ 'As for you, be on your guard. You will be handed over to the courts; you will be beaten in synagogues; you will be summoned to appear before governors and kings on my account to testify in their presence. ¹⁰ Before the end the gospel must be proclaimed to all nations. ¹¹ So when you are arrested and put on trial do not worry beforehand about what you will say, but when the time comes say whatever is given you to say, for it is not you who will be speaking, but the Holy Spirit. ¹² Brother will hand over brother to death, and a father

his child; children will turn against their parents and send them to their death. ¹³ Everyone will hate you for your allegiance to me, but whoever endures to the end will be saved.

¹⁴ 'But when you see "the abomination of desolation" usurping a place which is not his (let the reader understand), then those who are in Judaea must take to the hills. ¹⁵ If anyone is on the roof, he must not go down into the house to fetch anything out; ¹⁶ if anyone is in the field, he must not turn back for his coat. ¹⁷ Alas for women with child in those days, and for those who have children at the breast! ¹⁸ Pray that it may not come in winter. ¹⁹ For those days will bring distress such as there has never been before since the beginning of the world which God created, and will never be again. ²⁰ If the Lord had not cut short that time of troubles, no living thing could survive. However, for the sake of his own, whom he has chosen, he has cut short the time.

²¹ 'If anyone says to you then, "Look, here is the Messiah," or, "Look, there he is," do not believe it. ²² Impostors will come claiming to be messiahs or prophets, and they will produce signs and wonders to mislead, if possible, God's chosen. ²³ Be on your guard; I have forewarned you of it all.

²⁴ 'But in those days, after that distress,

the sun will be darkened,
the moon will not give her light;
²⁵ the stars will come falling from the sky,
the celestial powers will be shaken.

²⁶ 'Then they will see the Son of Man coming in the clouds with great power and glory, ²⁷ and he will send out the angels and gather his chosen from the four winds, from the farthest bounds of earth to the farthest bounds of heaven.

²⁸ 'Learn a lesson from the fig tree. When its tender shoots appear and are breaking into leaf, you know that summer is near. ²⁹ In the same way, when you see all this happening, you may know that the end is near, at the very door. ³⁰ Truly I tell you: the present generation will live to see it all. ³¹ Heaven and earth will pass away, but my words will never pass away.

³² 'Yet about that day or hour no one knows, not even the angels in heaven, not even the Son; no one but the Father.

³³ 'Be on your guard, keep watch. You do not know when the moment is coming. ³⁴ It is like a man away from home: he has left his house and

put his servants in charge, each with his own work to do, and he has ordered the door-keeper to stay awake. [35] Keep awake, then, for you do not know when the master of the house will come. Evening or midnight, cock-crow or early dawn – [36] if he comes suddenly, do not let him find you asleep. [37] And what I say to you, I say to everyone: Keep awake.'

One of the differences between Mark and the other three gospels is that Mark has few long speeches of Jesus. Matthew has five; Luke presents Jesus as a teacher and his book contains the well-known parables; John has the discourses, for example on the bread of life (in chapter 6), and at the supper (13 – 17); but Mark has only the collection of parables in chapter 4 and the answer to the question of the disciples (13.3–37) given to them on the mount of Olives.

The transition from the temple, the scene of the disputes, (mentioned at 11.27 and 12.41) to the mount of Olives is covered by the exclamation of one of the disciples: Look, Teacher, what huge stones! What fine buildings! Herod's restored temple was one of the seven wonders of the world; Jesus predicts its complete destruction (and this happened at the end of the war between the Jews and the Romans, in AD 70). The four disciples who had been mentioned by name at the beginning of the gospel (1.16–20) ask Jesus privately when this will be, and what signs there will be that it is about to happen. That provides the cue for the speech.

In Hebrew literature, and in Greek, famous characters make speeches towards the end of their lives, and the subject of these speeches is often what will happen in the future, after they have died. It must have been thought that old men, in their last days, were given the gift of prophesying, and could see how things would turn out. (See, for example, Jacob in Genesis 48 – 49, Joseph in Genesis 50, Moses in Deuteronomy 33, Joshua in Joshua 24, David in 2 Samuel 23 and 1 Chronicles 28, Mattathias in 1 Maccabees 2.)

The speech of Jesus at this point in Mark provides the readers with an explanation of a problem that the book will have raised in their minds. The first words of Jesus were that God would rule, and that it would happen soon. The book will end before that promise is fulfilled, so the readers are left with the question, When will this happen, and how shall we know that the end is coming? The emphasis in the speech is on what the disciples must not think: they must not think that the preliminary signs are the final signs; they must not be misled; they must not assume that every disaster is the final disaster. They must wait until all the lights in the sky have gone out, and only then will they see the Son of Man coming in the splendour in which he had been seen by three of these four disciples, at the Transfiguration.

That is to say, the most prominent characteristic of the speech is its negativity: the end is not yet; do not believe it. The temptation will be to think that events are so bad it must be the end. The speech refutes this; evil can get even worse, beyond anything you have ever imagined. Every sort of help or support will be withdrawn: there will be nobody you can rely on, and no stability in the world, or in the family, or among the followers of Christ. The darkness will become complete, both the literal darkness and the metaphorical. You must wait in patience, without seeing what you are waiting for; all there will be is disaster and distress. Then the Son of Man will come, and God's reign will begin.

One might have expected such a speech to have been placed at the end of the book, after the account of the crucifixion and resurrection, but not here, before the final events in Jerusalem have been described. By putting it here, however, Mark has provided his readers with the help they will undoubtedly need for understanding the account he is to write of the crucifixion of Jesus. Jesus will go into the darkness and destruction; he will be deserted by disciples, by family and (he will say) by God. We have known, since the middle of the book, that anyone who wants to be a disciple must follow Jesus (8.34); there is only one way, both for him and for them. Mark describes now, in chapter

13, the way as it will be for the disciples; and if they attend to what he says about that, now, they will not lose heart when they read what happens to Jesus in chapters 14 – 16. Both accounts will end in glory: the Son of Man coming and sending the angels to gather the chosen; and the resurrection of Jesus, who is no longer a corpse in a tomb.

The mount of Olives opposite the temple is the site for the speech, possibly because of the reference to it in Zechariah: On that day his feet will stand on the mount of Olives, which lies to the east of Jerusalem (14.4); Jesus foretells what will happen at the very place where it will happen.

The many false claimants who will say 'I am he' are contrasted with Jesus; in this gospel (unlike John) he only once says 'I am', and that is when he is questioned by the high priest (14.61; cf. 6.50), but then he has been arrested, bound, and is about to be condemned to death; it will not be so, one assumes, with the false claimants, who are saying it in order to gather followers around them; and, whereas Jesus (one might say) had no followers in the end, the false pretenders will have many. Success is no index of authenticity.

Political and natural disasters are only the preliminaries to the end, not the end itself; they are bound to happen (words that are a quotation from the book of Daniel [2.28], where they refer to the future that is determined by God and revealed by him to his servants). This is the context in which faith and hope must guide the disciples, as they are brought into court, beaten in synagogues, and made to stand before governors and kings.

One of the things that is bound to happen first, before the end of this age, is the preaching of the gospel. (It is uncertain whether Mark intended the words 'to all nations' to be taken with this sentence, or with the preceding sentence.) Even this is not to worry them; they are to say what is given to them; in the case of Jesus, as we shall see, he will say little and his silence will surprise Pilate; but others will speak for him, and they will speak the truth without meaning it, but in mockery. Micah's prophecy (7.6) about the divisions within families will be fulfilled. The disciples should expect nothing except hatred: but it must be hatred for the right reason, 'for your allegiance to me'; what he commands and what human beings want are opposed to each other; his way and theirs are incompatible; they are for acquisition, he for destruction. Destruction, however, is the road to salvation, and enduring destruction is the way to be saved.

The expression 'the abomination of desolation' is a quotation from Daniel (9.27 etc.) where it refers to the desecration of the altar in the temple in Jerusalem by the Greeks in 164 BC; it became a term used to describe a future event that would happen before the end of this age. Evil, it was thought, would have its greatest success, and would be worshipped as the god of the world. Disasters would become even greater, unprecedented and unrepeatable, so much so that God would intervene and shorten the time of waiting.

Even then, however, it will not be the time to believe that the Messiah or his prophet has come. There will still be impostors and false pretenders, and they will provide miracles as proofs that they are genuine. (Contrast Jesus, who refused to give a sign when asked for one [8.11ff.] and frequently commanded those whom he had healed to say nothing to anybody.)

Only when there is no light left, neither sun, nor moon, nor stars, and when the powers that control the world have been shaken, will the Son of Man come, and the rule of God begin; the elect will be gathered from all over the world, wherever the gospel has been preached and, like the seed in the good soil, has produced the crop that is to be harvested.

It is surprising that Mark makes no attempt to describe the life of the age to come. He has given us twenty-one verses (13.5–25) on the events leading up to the coming of the Son of Man, but only one on what will happen next: he will send out the angels and gather his chosen. Maybe he thought he had done as much as anyone could, in the earlier part of the book: the sick will be healed, the demoniacs set free, the lame cured, the unclean made holy, the hungry fed, the dead raised up; there will be no more storms and no more sea. The miracles tell us all we need to know:

it will not be as it is now; we can only know how it will be by contrast with how it is.

The parable of the fig tree, which has new leaves each year, relates the events described here to the end of this age: what fig leaves are to summer, the disasters that have been described will be to the coming of the Son of Man. Christians in the first century believed that Jesus had said that it would all happen in the lifetime of his contemporaries (9.1; though he refused to be more specific) and it did not. The set of ideas that Jesus grew up with included the expectation that God would intervene finally in the near future. There was, as far as we know, no crisis when the last of those who had been born before AD 30 (or whenever the crucifixion took place) died, without the end having come. Apocalyptic movements do not depend on the accuracy of their predictions, but have power to survive non-fulfilments and reform. We can see this happening in the books of the New Testament and the early Christian writings that came after them.

The final parable of the speech (which is also the final parable of the book) portrays the disciples as like the night-porter, the man whose whole work is to stay awake in order to be ready to open the door to the owner of the house when he returns. Paul had said that discipleship involved faith and love – and hope: faith in what God had done in raising Jesus from the dead; love for God and for the brethren; and hope, which is waiting for Christ's coming and enduring the evils of the present. In Mark, too, all the disciples are to obey what Jesus says to the four on the mount of Olives: Be ready; stay awake.

14.1–11 Passover, anointing and betrayal

It was two days before the festival of Passover and Unleavened Bread, and the chief priests and the scribes were trying to devise some

scheme to seize him and put him to death. ² 'It must not be during the festival,' they said, 'or we should have rioting among the people.'
³ Jesus was at Bethany, in the house of Simon the leper. As he sat at table, a woman came in carrying a bottle of very costly perfume, pure oil of nard. She broke it open and poured the oil over his head. ⁴ Some of those present said indignantly to one another, 'Why this waste? ⁵ The perfume might have been sold for more than three hundred denarii and the money given to the poor'; and they began to scold her. ⁶ But Jesus said, 'Leave her alone. Why make trouble for her? It is a fine thing she has done for me. ⁷ You have the poor among you always, and you can help them whenever you like; but you will not always have me. ⁸ She has done what lay in her power; she has anointed my body in anticipation of my burial. ⁹ Truly I tell you: wherever the gospel is proclaimed throughout the world, what she has done will be told as her memorial.'
¹⁰ Then Judas Iscariot, one of the Twelve, went to the chief priests to betray him to them. ¹¹ When they heard what he had come for, they were glad and promised him money; and he began to look for an opportunity to betray him.

Mark now begins his account of the suffering, death and resurrection of the Son of Man; Jesus had predicted it for the first time in the middle of the book (8.31), and again and again, both on the way to Jerusalem and, after they had arrived there, in the parable of the vineyard. We have, therefore, been told many times what is to happen, and been told by the one to whom it will happen; this means that we understand the events that follow, from here to the end of the book, as the destiny that is to be accepted by Jesus: what will happen is what was meant to happen.

In the introduction to the account, Mark will tell us something we had not known before this point: he will tell us now what he never mentions anywhere else in the book – what time of year it was. It was two days before the feast of Passover and Unleavened Bread. This explains why Jesus and the disciples have come up to Jerusalem: it was one of the festivals that had to be kept in the city. But Mark is much more interested in what will happen to Jesus while he is in Jerusalem, than in his reason for being there;

Passover will interpret his death and resurrection; it will be for Mark's readers their release from slavery. Paul had said, Christ our Passover lamb has been sacrificed (1 Corinthians 5.7).

The chief priests and the scribes, Mark says, were trying to seize Jesus deceitfully and kill him; not publicly or in a straightforward way. They had understood the parable of the vineyard and seen that it was aimed at them, and they know that Jesus is popular with the crowd. Their intention is not to arrest him during Passover, but they fail to fulfil it, and it turns out that Jesus is seized after he has given himself to the disciples at the supper, and during the night that commemorated the exodus from Egypt. God's will overrides human schemes, and their intentions are disposed of by him.

Mark follows the practice that he has already used so often in the gospel, of putting one story inside another: the plans of the authorities, in the first paragraph, will be advanced by Judas Iscariot, one of the Twelve, in the third paragraph. He goes to them in order to hand Jesus over to them; their scheme, they believe, will be achieved through his help to their satisfaction, and they promise to give him money for his part in it. Judas seeks (a word Mark always uses of wrong intentions) how to do this when the time is right, and, without understanding what he is doing, arranges the arrest at the time of the year that was most appropriate.

When Mark arranges two stories in this way, he means us to see one in the light of the other. (Compare temple and fig tree in chapter 11.) The account of the plan of the priests is not to be allowed to make us think that Jesus is simply at the mercy of sinners; though this is true, it is not the whole truth. The reality of the situation is that God's will is being done even though the actors in the drama do not know that this is so or intend that it should be so.

The woman, in the central paragraph of this section, anoints Jesus on his head with expensive ointment, as if he were a king. He is a king, as Mark will insist repeatedly in his account of the crucifixion; the title will come six times there, and nowhere else in the book. He is king by death, not by power; by what he suffers, not by what he does; by being destroyed, not by saving his life. Jesus defends her wasteful action on the grounds of an intention she did not have (as far as we are told), and says that she will be remembered for it all over the world, wherever the gospel is preached.

Mark does not inform us of the woman's own purpose, any more than he does of the motive of Judas Iscariot in going to the authorities. Their intentions are not part of the story, and have no place in it, as Mark conceives his work as the writer of a gospel. All we need to know is that Jesus was handed over to the agents of destruction by one of the Twelve, and that he was anointed for burial before he had died: a sign that his death was the most significant act in his life.

What will follow may read like tragedy, but Mark does not mean us to take it so. The reader who now knows Mark's mind (from the way in which the evangelist has prepared us for this part of his book) and who has caught Mark's sense of God's action within the realm of human sin and blindness, will not find his final pages depressing; they will contain good news of the way that leads to the kingdom of God.

14.12–31   The supper

¹² Now on the first day of Unleavened Bread, when the Passover lambs were being slaughtered, his disciples said to him, 'Where would you like us to go and prepare the Passover for you?' ¹³ So he sent off two of his disciples with these instructions: 'Go into the city, and a man will meet you carrying a jar of water. Follow him, ¹⁴ and when he enters a house give this message to the householder: "The Teacher says, 'Where is the room in which I am to eat the Passover with my disciples?' " ¹⁵ He will show you a large upstairs room, set out in readiness. Make the preparations for us there.' ¹⁶ Then the disciples

went off, and when they came into the city they found everything just as he had told them. So they prepared the Passover.

[17] In the evening he came to the house with the Twelve. [18] As they sat at supper Jesus said, 'Truly I tell you: one of you will betray me – one who is eating with me.' [19] At this they were distressed; and one by one they said to him, 'Surely you do not mean me?' [20] 'It is one of the Twelve', he said, 'who is dipping into the bowl with me. [21] The Son of Man is going the way appointed for him in the scriptures; but alas for that man by whom the Son of Man is betrayed! It would be better for that man if he had never been born.'

[22] During supper he took bread, and having said the blessing he broke it and gave it to them, with the words: 'Take this; this is my body.' [23] Then he took a cup, and having offered thanks to God he gave it to them; and they all drank from it. [24] And he said to them, 'This is my blood, the blood of the covenant, shed for many. [25] Truly I tell you: never again shall I drink from the fruit of the vine until that day when I drink it new in the kingdom of God.'

[26] After singing the Passover hymn, they went out to the mount of Olives. [27] And Jesus said to them, 'You will all lose faith; for it is written: "I will strike the shepherd and the sheep will be scattered." [28] Nevertheless, after I am raised I shall go ahead of you into Galilee.' [29] Peter answered, 'Everyone else may lose faith, but I will not.' [30] Jesus said to him, 'Truly I tell you: today, this very night, before the cock crows twice, you yourself will disown me three times.' [31] But Peter insisted: 'Even if I have to die with you, I will never disown you.' And they all said the same.

Two disciples are sent to prepare the Passover meal in Jerusalem, where it had to be eaten in the evening. The arrangements for meeting a man carrying a jar are mysterious and unexplained, and similar to the instructions for finding the colt for the entry into Jerusalem. Mark leaves us in no doubt that the meal will be the Passover, even though when he comes to describe the occasion there will be no reference to the lamb, the unleavened bread, the bitter herbs or the cups of wine that were all part of the festival. In place of that, Mark tells us of Jesus' prediction of betrayal by one of the Twelve, and none of them is sure he does not refer to him, but one by one they all say, Can it be me? No answer is given, except that what is to happen has been written in scripture, and is therefore God's will. That does not excuse the man who hands Jesus over to his destroyers; for him, it would be preferable never to have existed. At the end of the account of the supper Mark returns to the theme of failure; they will all sin and lose faith in Jesus, not only the one who betrays him. Zechariah's prophecy will be fulfilled: God will strike the shepherd and the sheep will be scattered (13.7). What is still to be narrated is to be understood in the light of this prophecy: Jesus' death is willed by God and the failure of the disciples is included in the divine foreknowledge and therefore within the scope of God's power to put it right. Jesus predicts how this will take place: God will raise him from the dead, and he will go ahead of them into Galilee. No further explanation is given, but the reader believes that Jesus has been raised to life after three days, and that he will come again as the judge and inaugurator of the reign of God.

Simon, whom Jesus had called the Rock, now distinguishes himself from the rest of the Twelve by refusing to accept the prediction: he will not fail. This only reveals that he will in fact be the worst of them all; he will disown Jesus three times before the cock crows twice in the morning. Peter insists that he would rather die with Jesus than disown him, and the rest of the Twelve say the same. Good intentions can be a snare and conceal the frailty of the will; we shall not be saved by thinking ourselves better than we are. We shall not, in fact, be saved by thinking anything, but by what is done for us, and thrust upon us without our understanding it. Mark has already told us this.

At the centre of Mark's account of the supper, in between the sayings about the disciples' failure, and instead of a description of the festal food they ate and the wine they drank, is the extraordinary and unexpected action of Jesus: he takes bread, thanks God and gives it to them, telling them to take it and saying that it is his body. He does the same with the cup: he takes it, gives thanks to God and gives it to them. They drink it, and only then does he tell them what it is they have done: they have drunk his blood, that is, they have taken responsibility for his death (compare 2 Samuel

23.17). What they have done, however, is what God means to happen; it will establish a new relationship between God and human beings; Jesus' death is for the benefit of others; he stands in and surrenders himself to God completely, loving God with all his heart, all his understanding, all his strength, and loving his neighbour as himself; he gives everything, whatever he has, his whole existence. He gives it to them, by his own death; he makes the disciples into those who eat his body and drink his blood; they are his consumers, that is, his destroyers, the real cause of his destruction.

The failure of the Twelve and their treachery (from Judas, the last in the list, to Simon Peter, the first, 3.16ff.; notice how Mark always adds, after the name Judas, the descriptive phrase, one of the Twelve) are part of the means by which they will be saved. This is the economy of God: he uses evil for his own good purposes; life is through death, and salvation through destruction; the covenant that brings fellowship with God is made with blood, and it is the blood of God's Son. This is the foolishness of God, that he uses the worst to make the best. The disciples do the worst that anyone could do, to a friend, a teacher, let alone the Messiah and their Lord. But the evil that they do is made into the means of their redemption, and Jesus goes to his death giving thanks to God as he passes them the bread, his body, and the cup, his blood. He is glad to do for them what they cannot do for themselves; though, as we shall see, the doing of it will remove from him all joy and confidence.

Jesus lays it down that his relationship with his followers is like that between food and those who eat it: we live at the expense of what we consume. It is a fact of which everybody is aware, that if we do not eat we cannot live. Mark's account of the supper applies this insight to our understanding of discipleship. It is not possible to follow Jesus in the way that he goes. The Twelve demonstrate that this is so, and the prophet had foretold it: the shepherd bears the brunt and the sheep are scattered. The faith that saves is the faith that accepts what must be. Mark is too subtle to put it like that. In his story, there is no preparation of the Twelve for their first communion; there is not even the explanatory saying before they receive the cup. Salvation is completed first, without comment, and faith and understanding come later and are never adequate or complete.

Jesus says that he will not drink wine again, until the kingdom of God comes. It is the last time he uses this expression in Mark's gospel (but not the last time it occurs in the book). Jesus takes a vow of abstinence from wine, to show what it is that will come as the result of his action. There will be a new age in which God will rule and there will be no more sin, or suffering, or evil of any kind, but it will all be joy and rejoicing, new wine, eternal life, seeing God and loving him. All this will happen because of the self-denial of Jesus, and that is still to be described.

14.32–52   Jesus is arrested

³² When they reached a place called Gethsemane, he said to his disciples, 'Sit here while I pray.' ³³ And he took Peter and James and John with him. Horror and anguish overwhelmed him, ³⁴ and he said to them, 'My heart is ready to break with grief; stop here, and stay awake.' ³⁵ Then he went on a little farther, threw himself on the ground, and prayed that if it were possible this hour might pass him by. ³⁶ 'Abba, Father,' he said, 'all things are possible to you; take this cup from me. Yet not my will but yours.'

³⁷ He came back and found them asleep; and he said to Peter, 'Asleep, Simon? Could you not stay awake for one hour? ³⁸ Stay awake, all of you; and pray that you may be spared the test. The spirit is willing, but the flesh is weak.' ³⁹ Once more he went away and prayed. ⁴⁰ On his return he found them asleep again, for their eyes were heavy; and they did not know how to answer him.

⁴¹ He came a third time and said to them, 'Still asleep? Still resting? Enough! The hour has come. The Son of Man is betrayed into the hands of sinners. ⁴² Up, let us go! The traitor is upon us.'

43 He was still speaking when Judas, one of the Twelve, appeared, and with him a crowd armed with swords and cudgels, sent by the chief priests, scribes, and elders. 44 Now the traitor had agreed with them on a signal: 'The one I kiss is your man; seize him and get him safely away.' 45 When he reached the spot, he went straight up to him and said, 'Rabbi,' and kissed him. 46 Then they seized him and held him fast.

47 One of the bystanders drew his sword, and struck the high priest's servant, cutting off his ear. 48 Then Jesus spoke: 'Do you take me for a robber, that you have come out with swords and cudgels to arrest me? 49 Day after day I have been among you teaching in the temple, and you did not lay hands on me. But let the scriptures be fulfilled.' 50 Then the disciples all deserted him and ran away.

51 Among those who had followed Jesus was a young man with nothing on but a linen cloth. They tried to seize him; 52 but he slipped out of the linen cloth and ran away naked.

Up to this point in the book, we have been told almost nothing about the emotions and inner feelings of Jesus; we might have thought of him as not having fear or sadness. Mark's description of Jesus might have left us aware only of his difference from us: his faith, confidence in God, clear sense of God's will and devotion to it; and this, in turn, might have led us to think of the death of Jesus as though it cost him nothing; that it came to him naturally, foreseen, expected and faithfully accepted. Mark now corrects any such possible misconception. The nearer Jesus comes to his death, the more overwhelmed he is by it; and the clearer this becomes to us, the more thankful we are to be for what he has done for us. Faith includes gratitude, and its extent in this case should be unfathomable.

Mark does not tell us at what point Judas detached himself from the Twelve; we shall only know that he has done so, when we see him arriving with the crowd from the Jewish authorities which has come to arrest Jesus. Jesus, on the other hand, separates himself from the disciples; they are told to sit; Peter, James and John are to stay awake; he goes further, to pray. He began,

Mark says, to be greatly distressed and troubled. The narrative is intended to draw our attention to this.

There have been occasions before on which a group of three or four disciples was taken aside from the rest, and some special revelation was given to them: the raising of the girl, in chapter 5; the glory of the Son of Man when he returns, in chapter 9; the events leading up to the end of this age, in chapter 13. Now, however, what is revealed is the thoughts and emotions of Jesus, as he goes to his destruction; and this is done by showing Jesus at prayer.

We have seen him praying before this, at night or in the early morning, always at a time of crisis; what is different about this occasion is that others are with him, and we are told what he said. He repeats a phrase that we have already heard in this book (9.23; 10.27): All things are possible to you. It is the prayer of one who believes in God. He addresses God as Abba, an Aramaic word that means Father. And he asks that the hour (of death) might pass him by, and that the cup (of suffering) might be taken from him. But then he surrenders himself to what God wills for him.

How could a father will the death of his son? There is a model for it, in the scriptures, when Abraham, in obedience to God, prepares to sacrifice his only son, Isaac. (The word 'only' was repeated in that story [Genesis 22] in the Greek translation; it is the same word that is used of Jesus in Mark 1.11, 9.7, 12.6.) This time there will be no reprieve and no substitution of a ram in place of the son. The Father does not spare his own Son, but gives him up for us all (Romans 8.32, quoting Genesis 22.16).

Jesus accepts this, in prayer before the Father; and its effect on him, as Mark presents the story, is to force him into silence and, in the end, into darkness and desolation. The effect on the three disciples is that they cannot even stay awake; they will therefore fall into temptation when the moment arrives. Jesus makes excuses for them: they do will what they should with the spirit, but the flesh fights against it; weakness overcomes good will, and prevents us from doing what we should.

The account of the repetition of the prayer and of the return to the disciples a second time and a third, emphasizes the separation that is now being made between Jesus and all the rest of humanity. The hour has come for the Son of Man to do and suffer what only he can do and suffer; and he goes to it willing it and accepting it. No one knows for certain the meaning of the Greek word that is translated 'Enough'; it could mean that the three-fold prayer and the three-fold failure of the disciples are all that is needed to show what time it is: the time for the one to die on behalf of the many.

The agreed signal by which the armed men will be able to identify Jesus is the kiss; in Greek, one word means both to kiss and to love. Judas, one of the Twelve, who should be a friend and whose kiss should signify affection, uses this gesture and no other to send Jesus to his death. By not attempting to tell us what Judas' motive had been, Mark allows us to identify ourselves with him; religious people no less than others bear responsibility for the death of Jesus and benefit from it. Judas acts for us in what he does and there are no innocent people. Jesus dies for all, even for his closest followers. Or, to put it another way, there are no followers now. The only person who kisses Jesus, in Mark, is the one of the Twelve who is the agent of his destruction. The only way we can love him is to kill him.

One of the bystanders (Mark does not say 'a disciple'; it is too late now to think that there are any) attempts to use force and is rebuked, by implication: Jesus is not a person who needs to be arrested by armed men; their weapons are inappropriate, and so is the bystander's drawn sword. Jesus must go in the way that the scriptures have said; he must die, and die alone. The departure of 'all' (the words 'the disciples' are not there in Greek) is thus, ironically, completely appropriate.

The situation is summed up in the story of the lad who leaves his one piece of clothing behind, preferring nakedness to being found with Jesus. This expresses the matter clearly. To be seen without your clothes was, in that society, the greatest shame imaginable; but even that was better than being in the company of Jesus on the night of his arrest. Not even the horror of being exposed was enough to overcome the fear of sharing in the hour, the cup, the desolation. We must let that alone; it costs more to redeem our souls than we can muster.

14.53–72   Jesus and Peter at the high priest's house

[53] Then they led Jesus away to the high priest's house, where the chief priests, elders, and scribes were all assembling. [54] Peter followed him at a distance right into the high priest's courtyard; and there he remained, sitting among the attendants and warming himself at the fire.

[55] The chief priests and the whole Council tried to find evidence against Jesus that would warrant a death sentence, but failed to find any. [56] Many gave false evidence against him, but their statements did not tally. [57] Some stood up and gave false evidence against him to this effect: [58] 'We heard him say, "I will pull down this temple, made with human hands, and in three days I will build another, not made with hands." ' [59] But even on this point their evidence did not agree.

[60] Then the high priest rose to his feet and questioned Jesus: 'Have you no answer to the accusations that these witnesses bring against you?' [61] But he remained silent and made no reply.

Again the high priest questioned him: 'Are you the Messiah, the Son of the Blessed One?' [62] 'I am,' said Jesus; 'and you will see the Son of Man seated at the right hand of the Almighty and coming with the clouds of heaven.' [63] Then the high priest tore his robes and said, 'Do we need further witnesses? [64] You have heard the blasphemy. What is your decision?' Their judgement was unanimous: that he was guilty and should be put to death.

[65] Some began to spit at him; they blindfolded him and struck him with their fists, crying out, 'Prophesy!' And the attendants slapped him in the face.

[66] Meanwhile Peter was still below in the courtyard. One of the high priest's servant-girls came by [67] and saw him there warming himself.

101

> She looked closely at him and said, 'You were with this man from Nazareth, this Jesus.' [68] But he denied it: 'I know nothing,' he said; 'I have no idea what you are talking about,' and he went out into the forecourt. [69] The servant-girl saw him there and began to say again to the bystanders, 'He is one of them'; [70] and again he denied it.
>
> Again, a little later, the bystanders said to Peter, 'You must be one of them; you are a Galilean.' [71] At this he started to curse, and declared with an oath, 'I do not know this man you are talking about.' [72] At that moment the cock crowed for the second time; and Peter remembered how Jesus had said to him, 'Before the cock crows twice, you will disown me three times.' And he burst into tears.

Mark has two stories to tell in this section, and again he puts one inside the other; this time, the two events are the opposite of each other, one being a confession of faith, and the other a denial of it; one, an account of someone saying very little, the other, of a person who speaks too much; one dies for what he says, and the other escapes with his life, and weeps.

We have been warned what to expect of Peter: Today, this very night, before the cock crows twice, you yourself will disown me three times. Peter had refused to listen, trusting himself and not what had been said to him; he will, therefore, fulfil what has been foretold. Mark hints at what is to come when he says that Peter followed Jesus 'at a distance'; it is a warning in Mark of danger to come; he will use it again of the women at the crucifixion. Meanwhile, the scene is set for Peter's last appearance in the book: he is in the high priest's courtyard, seated with the high priest's attendants, and warming himself at their fire: visible to those who are part of the opposition to Jesus. Mark keeps us waiting for the dénouement.

The responsibility of all the Jewish authorities – chief priests, elders and scribes, the whole Council – is emphasized. They all agree to put Jesus to death, and so they all look for evidence that will warrant his execution. Mark's reason for saying this may be that, by the time he was writing and in the area for which he was writing, the separation between the synagogues and the churches had become complete; Paul had been so sure that Gentile Christians should not keep the Mosaic law, no other outcome would have been possible.

It is unlikely that Mark had information about a trial before the Council, or that such an occasion would have been possible on the night of Passover. Disciples could testify that Jesus had been arrested, and that he had been crucified (though they had not been present themselves); for most of the narrative between arrest and death, Mark would have had to turn to scripture, to what he believed must happen to fulfil the prophets.

Frequently in the Psalms the writer complains about false witnesses, and Mark takes that as a prediction of what happened to Jesus. He uses the idea in a subtle way: there were false witnesses; they testified that Jesus had said that he would destroy the temple (rebuilt by Herod), and replace it with another, made by God, in three days; their testimony did not agree, so the Council did not proceed with this charge. Mark has thus achieved the following affirmations: Scripture was fulfilled; the false witnesses spoke the truth without realizing it; Jesus will soon bring an end to Judaism; but that was not the reason why he was condemned by the Council: he was condemned for saying who he was.

The silence of Jesus, both here and in Pilate's court, fulfils a prophecy in Isaiah (He did not open his mouth, 53.7), but it is more than that; it is part of Mark's presentation of this day (Thursday evening to Friday evening) as the day when everything is back to front and upside down. Jesus had previously led us to expect that those who were arrested and put on trial would be given what to say (13.11); he is given nothing, that is why he is silent.

The high priest then uses two expressions that, in the sense that they are used here, became current at a later time mainly among the followers of Jesus. 'The Messiah' and 'the Son of the Blessed One' (meaning 'the Son of God'), though they have a pre-history in Judaism, became technical terms to express faith in Jesus among his disciples; it is unlikely that the high priest would use

103

them, or that they were even available at this time in the sense
that he is said to have used them. Mark's meaning is that Jesus
was put to death, not for something he had said about the temple,
but for saying who he was: only at this point in the book does
Jesus do this; it was essential to Mark's account of the crucifixion
that we should know that Jesus believed this about himself.
There would have been no force in mocking him as Messiah if
that was not who he thought he was.

Jesus says, I am, and provides the evidence: You (plural) will
see the fulfilment of what had been foretold by David (Psalm
110.1) and Daniel (7.13): the Son of Man will be seated at God's
right hand, accepted and approved by him; and he will come in
glory to judge the world. The evidence, that is to say, is only
available to those who believe, because it lies in the future, 'You
will see'. Verification of faith is always and only eschatological, in
the end. Christianity, from the first, was expressed in terms of
faith, love and hope: hope is faith with reference to the future, so
it cannot be proved, or disproved, now.

The spitting and the slaps to the face (literally, 'blows') are
probably included because of a passage in the prophets:

> I offered my back to the lash
> and my cheeks to blows,
> I did not hide my face from insult and spitting.
>> (Isaiah 50.6 in the Greek translation)

Though he is called upon to speak ('Prophesy!') he has nothing to
say; and indeed there is nothing to say in this situation. It is a time
for silence.

Mark has still to give us the rest of the story of Peter; knowing
what will happen in advance makes it no more acceptable, it only
increases the tension in the reader's mind. Mark picks up where
he had left off: Peter is looking after himself – warming himself.
A servant-girl puts the question, and all she asks is if Peter was
with the man from Nazareth, this Jesus. Peter cannot admit that
much (not that he was a disciple, the first of the disciples, the

Rock) even to a person who had no authority or power to injure him. The girl repeats the accusation to others, not to members of the Council, but to people who happened to be around in the forecourt; the whole matter is very low-key, and that makes it all the worse, and all the more poignant for the readers: we might cope with the great occasion, an appearance in court; it is the conversation on the bus that is the trouble. The unnamed by-standers argue (illogically) that, because Peter is from Galilee, he must be 'one of them'. Peter then declares with an oath, swearing by all that is true, on his honour, that he has nothing to do with the person they are talking about. Peter himself does not name him (perhaps meaning that he does not even know so much as the man's name); the girl names Jesus, no one else. There is the second cock-crow, and Peter remembers and weeps.

This is his last appearance; he is mentioned as one to whom the message of the resurrection must be given, but the women do not obey the young man who told them to do it. The ministry of the church, represented by Peter (and Judas, and the rest of the Twelve), for all its authority and importance, is cut down to size; the first apostle is singled out to be exhibited as supremely faithless. But all of this is part of a book that is good news: if one has died for all, then it does not matter that they are as miserable and contemptible as this; it only serves to increase our amazement and gratitude.

15.1–20a Jesus at the Praetorium

As soon as morning came, the whole Council, chief priests, elders, and scribes, made their plans. They bound Jesus and led him away to hand him over to Pilate. ² 'Are you the king of the Jews?' Pilate asked him. 'The words are yours,' he replied. ³ And the chief priests brought many charges against him. ⁴ Pilate questioned him again: 'Have you nothing to say in your defence? You see how many charges they are bringing against you.' [5] But, to Pilate's astonishment, Jesus made no further reply.

[6] At the festival season the governor used to release one prisoner requested by the people. [7] As it happened, a man known as Barabbas was then in custody with the rebels who had committed murder in the rising. [8] When the crowd appeared and began asking for the usual favour, [9] Pilate replied, 'Would you like me to release the king of the Jews?' [10] For he knew it was out of malice that Jesus had been handed over to him. [11] But the chief priests incited the crowd to ask instead for the release of Barabbas. [12] Pilate spoke to them again: 'Then what shall I do with the man you call king of the Jews?' [13] They shouted back, 'Crucify him!' [14] 'Why, what wrong has he done?' Pilate asked; but they shouted all the louder, 'Crucify him!' [15] So Pilate, in his desire to satisfy the mob, released Barabbas to them; and he had Jesus flogged, and then handed him over to be crucified.

[16] The soldiers took him inside the governor's residence, the Praetorium, and called the whole company together. [17] They dressed him in purple and, plaiting a crown of thorns, placed it on his head. [18] Then they began to salute him: 'Hail, king of the Jews!' [19] They beat him about the head with a stick and spat at him, and then knelt and paid homage to him. [20] When they had finished their mockery, they stripped off the purple robe and dressed him in his own clothes.

Jesus, as we have already noticed, has not been given anything to say, other than 'I am' to the high priest's question. To Pilate's questioning, his only reply is, in literal translation, You are speaking. But in a sense, it is not Pilate who speaks, but the Holy Spirit, as Jesus had promised (13.11); the Spirit speaks through Pilate, and tells us who Jesus is. Pilate uses an expression, The king of the Jews, which has been kept by Mark for this day, when it will be used repeatedly. Jesus had said that Gentile rulers lorded it over their subjects, but that it was not so with the disciples; there, the Son of Man gave his life as a ransom for many (10.42ff.). This was the way in which he could be recognized as the Son of Man. Pilate asks if Jesus is the king of the Jews, and if it follows that Jesus is put to death, we shall know that he is.

This is the only issue that matters; neither Mark nor his readers were interested in any charges brought by the chief priests. The overriding question is, Who is Jesus?, and the most reliable way to answer it is to see what he does.

What he does is suggested immediately: a man with an odd name, Barabbas (Son of the Father; Mark has told us that Bar means 'Son' [10.46] and that Abba means 'Father' [14.36]), a prisoner, rebel and murderer, is released by Pilate. Mark says it was a custom for the governor to do this at Passover, though there is no evidence, apart from the gospels, for such a custom, and Mark's historical accuracy is frequently questioned on this point. It would indeed be appropriate to the season, because Passover celebrated Israel's release from captivity in Egypt; but it would be uncharacteristic of Roman governors, and of Pilate in particular, a notoriously cruel person. Mark may have intended his readers to see it like this: Christ is our Passover; he sets us free from evil and death; we are sons and daughters of the Father, so our representative figure is Barabbas, whose name is a blank cheque on which we can write our own.

The crowd asks for Barabbas, not for Jesus; they ask for someone who is one of their own, and, as we also see it, our man. But this can only happen if Jesus is put to death: the custom, Mark says, was to release one prisoner. Jesus is put to death, not for any wrong he has done; Pilate asks them to be precise, but they refuse; he is put to death, in order that Barabbas may be released. Pilate's desire to please the crowd leads to the fulfilment of God's will as Jesus had predicted it (10.34). Jesus is flogged, and will be crucified.

The title 'king' is used six times in the description of the events of this Friday; first of all three times by Pilate, who means it as a kind of joke against the Jews. The Roman soldiers then take up the theme: they dress Jesus in purple, the emperor's colour; they make him a crown (of thorns), like the crowns of the emperors on the Roman coins of the time; and they salute him, Hail, king of the Jews! (In Greek, one word could be used to mean both emperor and king.) All of this is intended by the soldiers to be in jest: they combine beating and spitting with kneeling and paying homage. Then Jesus is dressed in his own clothes; Mark tells us this, because his clothes will be referred to again, and scripture will be fulfilled.

Jesus is now no longer the subject of Mark's sentences; he is the one to whom things are done, not the doer. Grammatically speaking, he is generally referred to from now to the end of this chapter in either the accusative or the dative case. He is to be seen now as the Saviour, but the Saviour is the one who is acted upon: he is sinned against, and thus destroyed. What Mark believes is that the one who is destroyed in this way is the destroyer of sin. Paul's interpretation will explain Mark's narrative: Christ was innocent of sin, and yet for our sake God made him one with human sinfulness, so that in him we might be made one with the righteousness of God (2 Corinthians 5.21).

15.20b–39   The crucifixion

Then they led him out to crucify him. ²¹ A man called Simon, from Cyrene, the father of Alexander and Rufus, was passing by on his way in from the country, and they pressed him into service to carry his cross.

²² They brought Jesus to the place called Golgotha, which means 'Place of a Skull', ²³ and they offered him drugged wine, but he did not take it. ²⁴ Then they fastened him to the cross. They shared out his clothes, casting lots to decide what each should have.

²⁵ It was nine in the morning when they crucified him; ²⁶ and the inscription giving the charge against him read, 'The King of the Jews'. ²⁷ Two robbers were crucified with him, one on his right and the other on his left.

²⁹ The passers-by wagged their heads and jeered at him: 'Bravo!' they cried, 'So you are the man who was to pull down the temple, and rebuild it in three days! ³⁰ Save yourself and come down from the cross.' ³¹ The chief priests and scribes joined in, jesting with one another: 'He saved others,' they said, 'but he cannot save himself. ³² Let the Messiah, the king of Israel, come down now from

the cross. If we see that, we shall believe.' Even those who were crucified with him taunted him.

[33] At midday a darkness fell over the whole land, which lasted till three in the afternoon; [34] and at three Jesus cried aloud, 'Eloï, Eloï, lema sabachthani?' which means, 'My God, my God, why have you forsaken me?' [35] Hearing this, some of the bystanders said, 'Listen! He is calling Elijah.' [36] Someone ran and soaked a sponge in sour wine and held it to his lips on the end of a stick. 'Let us see', he said, 'if Elijah will come to take him down.' [37] Then Jesus gave a loud cry and died; [38] and the curtain of the temple was torn in two from top to bottom. [39] When the centurion who was standing opposite him saw how he died, he said, 'This man must have been a son of God.'

Mark is describing a paradoxical situation. The one whom the wind and the sea obey is revealed in his powerlessness; the one who called disciples to be with him is now completely alone as far as they are concerned. (Mark will say that there were women there, but not until after he has told us that Jesus has died.) The absence of the Twelve is stressed by the coincidence that the man who is forced to carry the cross for Jesus is also called Simon, and that the places on the right and on the left of Jesus are occupied, not by James and John, who had said that they could share his baptism and his cup, but by a pair of robbers who, like Simon of Cyrene, are there involuntarily. The title 'king' comes for the fifth time in the notice that stated what the charge was, for which he was being crucified: he is being put to death only for what he is; and it is by being put to death that he is what he says: the one who gives his life. The psalm (22.18) is being fulfilled in the sharing of his clothes and the casting of lots to decide what each should have.

He was offered drugged wine (again an allusion to a psalm, 69.21) but he refused it, because he had to make no concessions; it was necessary for his followers to know that he had set himself to be wholly for them, without any holding back. As with the widow, it must be everything, whatever he had, the whole of his life.

The passers-by who jeer and wag their heads echo Psalm 22 again: All who see me jeer at me, grimace at me and wag their heads (verse 7).

Almost everything that is said during the crucifixion is true (as the readers understand it) but it is said in order to mock Jesus. There is no description of his physical suffering: no reference to nails or ropes to fasten him to the cross; no mention of wounds or blood; no cry of thirst; the word 'suffer' does not occur. No doubt Mark's first readers knew all about crucifixion, from seeing it constantly. If, however, Mark were asked the question, How did Jesus die?, his answer might be, He was mocked to death. All the emphasis in this section of the gospel is on the infliction of mental, not physical, suffering.

The kind of mockery that is most effective is that which is nearest to the truth. (No one is hurt by being mocked for what they know they cannot do: the most bitter ridicule is about that in which we thought we were competent.) This is why it was necessary for Mark to tell us that Jesus said 'I am', to the high priest's question. He is the one who will replace Herod's temple with another. He has said that he will be raised after three days. If he were to save himself, he would in fact only destroy himself; and he would not save anyone else. It is true that he cured others of their illnesses, he saved them; it is also true that he cannot save himself. His teaching has rebounded on him; he has only himself to blame. The mockers speak the truth, meaning only to ridicule Jesus, but bearing witness to him unintentionally. The sixth and final instance of the title 'king' is in the words of the chief priests and scribes; previously, those who have used the word in this section of the gospel have been Gentiles, and they have said, The king of the Jews; Jews apparently spoke of themselves as Israelites, not as Jews; so what the chief priests and scribes say is, Let the Messiah, the king of Israel, come down from the cross.

If we see that, they say, we shall believe. But what would they believe? Not what Mark's readers, or any other disciples of Jesus, believe. Not the gospel. Not that one died for all.

110

At the time of the Exodus, there had been darkness for three days over the whole land of Egypt, before the final plague, the death of the firstborn (Exodus 10.21ff.); now, there is darkness for three hours, and then God's firstborn will die. He speaks the first words of Psalm 22, the psalm that has been quoted and alluded to already. These are his last words in Mark's gospel, the main character's exit line; none of the other gospel writers followed Mark in this, but they all concluded with last words of Jesus that expressed power, victory and glory. It is characteristic of Mark not to do this: what we are given is the suffering; the glory is for faith and hope.

'Eloi' is misunderstood (perhaps deliberately; that would fit the irony of Mark's passion narrative) as though it were 'Elia', that is, 'Elijah', the one who was thought to deliver the righteous from danger. Elijah had, it was believed, set up an experiment to prove that the Lord was God, not Baal (1 Kings 18). Someone now tries to repeat the experiment on Jesus: he is given the drink, and they say, Let us see if Elijah will come to take him down from the cross. If Elijah comes, Jesus is who he says he is; if Elijah does not come, he is not. Jesus dies, without the intervention of Elijah, thus proving to those who think in this way that he was not the Messiah, the king of Israel. (It is possible that the centurion's words should be taken in this sense: He really was God's son! Of course not! There is a parallel in Greek between what the people said on Mount Horeb after Elijah's miracle: Truly the Lord is God; and what is said here, Truly this man was the Son of God. There is also the possibility that 'this man' should be translated 'this fellow', disparagingly, as in Acts 6.13.) Whatever Mark means the centurion to have thought, the readers or hearers of the book believe in Jesus as God's agent, because he died for them, bearing their sins.

One sign follows the death of Jesus; the curtain that divided the sanctuary from the rest of the temple was torn from top to bottom. Mark has taken great care to tell the story in such a way that the ambiguity of it is never lost or destroyed. The gospel is not obviously good news; a crucified man is not wisdom or a miracle, which is what Jews and Gentiles want (1 Corinthians 1.22ff.). The tearing of the veil could be taken in either of two ways: God's anger with his people, or his anger with Jesus. The reader is left to decide.

15.40–47 The burial

[40] A number of women were also present, watching from a distance. Among them were Mary of Magdala, Mary the mother of James the younger and of Joses, and Salome, [41] who had all followed him and looked after him when he was in Galilee, and there were many others who had come up to Jerusalem with him.

[42] By this time evening had come; and as it was the day of preparation (that is, the day before the sabbath), [43] Joseph of Arimathaea, a respected member of the Council, a man who looked forward to the kingdom of God, bravely went in to Pilate and asked for the body of Jesus. [44] Pilate was surprised to hear that he had died so soon, and sent for the centurion to make sure that he was already dead. [45] And when he heard the centurion's report, he gave Joseph leave to take the body. [46] So Joseph bought a linen sheet, took him down from the cross, and wrapped him in the sheet. Then he laid him in a tomb cut out of the rock, and rolled a stone against the entrance. [47] And Mary of Magdala and Mary the mother of Joses were watching and saw where he was laid.

The disciples had fled when Jesus was arrested, and though Peter had followed at a distance, we hear no more of him, nor of Judas. Mark has no disciples present during the crucifixion: the one of whom it was said that Jesus loved him, had not become a follower (10.21–22). But the isolation of Jesus, necessary though it was for Mark's theology (a ransom for many) created a problem for his narrative: who witnessed the crucifixion, the burial, and the finding of the empty tomb? He turns again to the Psalms, and recalls Psalm 38:

> My friends and companions shun me in my sickness,
> and my kinsfolk keep far off. (verse 11; in Greek 'far
> off' is the same as Mark's 'from a distance')

Of the three women who are mentioned by name, the second is referred to first as Mary the mother of James and Joses, then as Mary the mother of Joses, and finally as Mary the mother of James. A possible explanation of this is that she is Mary the mother of Jesus, mentioned in chapter 6, where the brothers of Jesus include James and Joses. And if it seems strange that Mark should refer to her in this roundabout way, we remember that Jesus had said, Who are my mother and my brothers? ... Here are my mother and my brothers (3.33–34). His followers are his family.

If we expect better things from the women than the men, Mark will disappoint us. In the end, they will go out of the story fleeing, in the same way as the disciples in Gethsemane (14.50, 52; 16.8).

Only now, when it is almost over, does Mark tell us what day of the week it is: Friday, the day on which one prepared for the sabbath. Jesus' disciples, unlike John the Baptist's, do not see to the burial of their master, but in their place comes Joseph of Arimathea, a member of the Council, who also looked forward to the kingdom of God, as Jesus had done. Jesus had spoken of it thirteen times in Mark's book, now we have the fourteenth and final instance of the expression. Jesus had said it was coming soon, but he died without seeing it. Joseph looks forward to it, and asks for the body of Jesus. Instead of a body (*sōma* in Greek), he is given a corpse (*ptōma*), when Pilate is certain that Jesus is dead and the centurion has assured him that this is so. It is Mark's final reminder that there is no way that leads to life, except by death, and that the death that brings us to life is the death of Jesus. Paul asked the Romans, Have you forgotten that when we were baptized into union with Christ Jesus we were baptized into his death? By that baptism into his death we were buried with him ... (6.3–4).

The burial was in a tomb cut out of a rock with a stone against the opening (a huge stone, Mark will say later). No one could enter except by moving the stone. Two of the women saw the place where he was buried, so there need be no doubt; they did not go to the wrong tomb on Easter morning, and the body could not easily have been stolen.

16.1–8   The empty tomb

When the sabbath was over, Mary of Magdala, Mary the mother of James, and Salome bought aromatic oils, intending to go and anoint him; [2] and very early on the first day of the week, just after sunrise, they came to the tomb. [3] They were wondering among themselves who would roll away the stone for them from the entrance to the tomb, [4] when they looked up and saw that the stone, huge as it was, had been rolled back already. [5] They went into the tomb, where they saw a young man sitting on the right-hand side, wearing a white robe; and they were dumbfounded. [6] But he said to them, 'Do not be alarmed; you are looking for Jesus of Nazareth, who was crucified. He has been raised; he is not here. Look, there is the place where they laid him. [7] But go and say to his disciples and to Peter: "He is going ahead of you into Galilee: there you will see him, as he told you."' [8] Then they went out and ran away from the tomb, trembling with amazement. They said nothing to anyone, for they were afraid.

We do not have the original manuscript that Mark wrote, only copies made from other copies, years later. Two of these later Greek texts of Mark end at 16.8, where Mark says that the women said nothing to anyone, for they were afraid. (One of these manuscripts is in the British Library, and the other in the Vatican Library.) Other manuscripts of Mark have a longer ending, verses 9 to 20; or a short ending consisting of a single verse. It is generally agreed that neither the short ending nor the long ending was written by Mark; some writers have suggested that Mark meant to stop with the silence, fear, and flight of the women.

If that was so, then the story ends with the announcement that Jesus has been raised from the dead; his corpse is no longer in the tomb, but he will be seen by his disciples, and Peter, in Galilee, as he had told them.

He had said to the four, Peter, James, John and Andrew, Then they will see the Son of Man coming in the clouds with great power and glory (13.26); and to the Council, You will see the Son of Man seated at the right hand of the Almighty and coming with the clouds of heaven (14.62).

The book ends where it began, looking forward to the time when God will rule on the earth. Nevertheless, in typically Marcan style, it ends with a final account of human failure. The women should not have been coming on this, the third day; he had said, three times, that he would rise again (8.31; 9.31; 10.34). They were wrong to think that they needed to anoint his body; he had said that the woman at Bethany had done it (14.8). They need not have worried about moving the stone; it had been moved for them, before they arrived.

Mark goes out of his way to de-emphasize the resurrection, in case it take away from the significance of the death of Jesus. He describes the person who speaks the last words of the book as a young man, wearing a white robe; he does not call him an angel. The women are invited to see the place where the body had been put, but Mark does not say that they did so, or that the grave-clothes were still there. All he gives us is the statement that Jesus has been raised and that he will be seen. Those who hear the book will believe, or they will not; Mark puts no pressure on them. Faith cannot be forced.

The women who had expected to find a dead body and to perform final burial rites on a life that had ended, depart in fear and silence, disobeying the young man's words. The implications of what he had said were such that it would be better not to believe him. If Jesus really was God's Son, and all that he had said was true, there could be no going back to the past as it had been; to enter the kingdom of God it would be necessary to undergo much suffering.

Retrospect

Mark's gospel raises many questions, certainly for the twentieth-century reader; but it seems it was problematic also, at the time when it was originally produced in the first century. For example, some readers wanted to know what happened next, after the flight of the women from the tomb; and the longer and the shorter endings were written to satisfy them. The other three gospels, Matthew, Luke and John, were intended either to complement Mark by giving more information about Jesus, particularly about his teaching, or (and this seems more likely) to replace Mark with books thought to be more satisfactory for the needs of the churches. The earliest gospel was almost edged out by the later ones: copied less frequently, quoted less often, and seldom made the subject of a commentary. Its rediscovery is a nineteenth- and twentieth-century phenomenon.

One question that inevitably occurs to us is, How accurate is it, as a historical report? How much of Mark's account is a report of things said and done, just as they happened, and how much is it legend, that is, stories told to convey a meaning other than the factual and historical?

This does not seem to have been a problem for readers in the first century. The re-writing of the gospels shows that the main question was not, Did this happen?, but, What does it mean? Interpretation was more important than fact, and facts could be altered to produce new interpretations. We can see this in, for example, the changed order of paragraphs in the different gospels, and the alterations to the wording, even in those parts of the narrative where we might have expected them to preserve one form, and only one: the Lord's Prayer, the beatitudes, Peter's confession, the words of Jesus at the last supper and during the crucifixion.

Some of Mark's historical statements can be checked against the earliest Christian author whose writings have survived, the apostle Paul. He knew that Jesus was born of a woman, that he had twelve disciples one of whom was called Peter, and that he had brothers, one of whom was James; he knew the tradition of the supper on the night Jesus was betrayed, and that Jesus died by crucifixion, was buried, and was believed to have been raised to life and seen by various (mostly male) witnesses. Paul's expectation that Jesus would soon return as the judge of the living and the dead, and that God would put all enemies under his feet, and that in the end God would be all in all, matches exactly Mark's account of Jesus proclaiming the kingdom of God as an event that would happen soon.

Two elements in Mark, however, are not to be found in Paul's surviving letters: we should have had no idea from Paul that Jesus used parables; and we should not have known that he healed the sick or that he did other miracles.

The historicity of Mark's account of the miracles must be the area in which there will be the greatest disagreement, and it will be difficult to find objective criteria to reach a decision about them. Exorcisms and healings were believed to happen at that time and in that society; miracles of walking on water, feeding multitudes as Mark describes them, and raising the dead will seem to some people more of the nature of legends: very important for understanding what the people who told the stories believed about Jesus, but not to be taken as straightforward accounts of what happened. (Mark's own emphasis on secrecy about some of the healings, and on the absence of miracles at the end of the book, means that the main thrust of his message would not be impaired if the miracles had not happened.)

Another historical question that Mark's gospel raises concerns Jesus' claims about himself: Did he say who he was? Did he believe he was different from other people, God's only Son?

Mark represents him as using the expression 'The Son of Man' as a title referring to himself, but recent studies have raised questions about whether this can have been what actually happened. There is, apparently, no evidence that other people used the expression in this way; no one is said to have written about the coming Son of Man. Mark does not often describe Jesus as using other titles: Christ, Son, Prophet. But this does not mean that Jesus did not think and act in a way that would only have been possible if he had believed that it was the last days, and that he had a mission to proclaim God's coming rule and call people to enter it by associating with him. In his use of titles, Mark is only making explicit what was almost certainly implicit in the words and acts of Jesus.

On the other hand, it seems that Mark has presented a picture of Jesus as one who clashed with Pharisees and scribes and others in Judaism, in a way that exaggerates the difference between him and them. First-century Judaism consisted of a wide range of opinions, and it is now thought that Jesus was within the limits of what was accepted. Mark's account overdoes the conflicts; Jesus was an observant Jew, and so were his original disciples and family and the church in Jerusalem of which they were members. Mark has probably painted his portrait of Jesus with colours taken from Paul.

This leads on to the hotly debated issue of the trials of Jesus before the Council and Pilate, the reason he was put to death, and who was responsible for the decision to execute him. Here again it looks as though Mark has transferred the blame to the Jews, whereas in fact it was the Romans who acted, in an attempt to keep the peace in Jerusalem during a difficult festival season.

All of this is to say that one of the areas in which Mark may give a lop-sided account is to do with his representation of the Jews; we can see in his book the beginning of an anti-Jewish tendency that increases in Matthew, John, and later Christian writers. It was almost inevitable at some stage, because the Way began as an entirely Jewish movement, and then broke away from its parent. There had to be conflict with Judaism, in order to establish the separate identity of the offspring.

A question of a different kind altogether, but inevitable for any present-day reader of Mark, is: Does not the fact that the kingdom of God did not come, and still has not come, make the whole book totally useless? The message of Jesus was: God is going to rule; and he did not; how can one pay any attention to anything in a book that is so wrong on the central issue?

One thing that must be said is that Christianity survived the non-occurrence of the end. It evidently did not depend on the fulfilment of the expectation of Christ's immediate return for its continuance. It could adapt apocalyptic to new uses. One example of this is the Lord's Prayer, which originally seems to have been a petition for God to rule on the earth and for those who prayed it to be included in his kingdom, soon, today. But the prayer has continued to be used, without this interpretation. Another example of the ability of Christians to re-formulate their beliefs in a different mode, avoiding apocalyptic, is the gospel according to John. The emphasis shifted from: He will come, to, He is with us.

It is not totally impossible, we hope, to put ourselves into the world of a different age and think their thoughts; we do it, as far as we can, with other literature from the past, and the New Testament presents no greater problem than many other writings that come from other ages. It would be impossible to have books that did not reflect the age in which they were written; and the belief that God must intervene soon was the way many people in Judaism thought at the time of Jesus, including, no doubt, Jesus himself.

The final question which must arise for anyone reading Mark is, Is not the book far too negative? Jesus goes to his death in darkness and desolation, and predicts terrible disasters, through which his disciples must follow him. They are to expect destruction and welcome it: they must abandon everything.

Certainly Mark distinguishes self-abandonment from suicide; the disciples are to give up everything 'for my sake and for the gospel's', and this provides a context and criterion. Self-slaughter would not fit or pass this test. But even so, granted that they are not to seek martyrdom or to try to cause it to happen to them, is not the book excessively negative in its teaching, even, it has been suggested, masochistic?

There are, Jesus says, two commandments, and they are both about love, *agapē*. God is to be loved with all one's power, and one's neighbour is to be loved as oneself (which may likewise mean without any restrictions). The apparent negativity of the book is the other side of its positive teaching: if the demands that God and our neighbour make upon us are unlimited, there can be no scope for self-love and all that flows from it. It is one thing to say that Mark's message is hard to accept; it is not the same to say that we cannot assent to its truth. The good news must be more than we can accept. It was entirely appropriate that Mark should end his gospel with the women's fear and silence.

Books on Mark's gospel

Mark's gospel, like John's, continues to attract the attention of writers, and the number of books and articles that appear every year is immense. The purpose of this note is simply to provide a starting point for anyone who has no previous knowledge of the subject or of the literature that there is concerning it.

One area on which information may be required is that of the Synoptic problem; that is, the relationship between the first three gospels. All introductions to the New Testament will have a chapter on this subject, and there is an excellent, informative and judicious article by C. M. Tuckett in *A Dictionary of Biblical Interpretation*, edited by R. J. Coggins and J. L. Hauldon (SCM Press, 1990), 'Synoptic problem', which includes a brief and useful bibliography. Other articles in this book are also relevant, e.g. 'Source criticism', 'Mark, Gospel of', 'Messianic secret', 'Kingdom of God'.

A commentary on Mark which is particularly strong on the historical problems that the book raises is D. E. Nineham, *Saint Mark* in the Pelican Gospel Commentaries (Penguin Books, 1963). For a commentary that has taken account of the study of Mark since the 1960s, there is M. D. Hooker, *The Gospel According to Saint Mark* in Black's New Testament Commentaries (A. & C. Black, 1991), and a longer and more recent book by R. H. Gundry, *Mark: A Commentary on His Apology for the Cross* (Eerdmans, Grand Rapids, 1993).

The following can also be recommended as books that have in various ways helped the present writer and may explain at greater length some of the problems dealt with more briefly above:

R. H. Lightfoot, *History and Interpretation in the Gospels* (Hodder and Stoughton, 1935)

R. H. Lightfoot, *Locality and Doctrine in the Gospels* (Hodder and Stoughton, 1938)

R. H. Lightfoot, *The Gospel Message of St Mark* (Oxford University Press, 1950)

A. M. Farrer, *A Study in St Mark* (Dacre Press, 1951)

T. Weedon, *Mark – Traditions in Conflict* (Westminster Press, 1971)

D. Rhoads and D. Michie, *Mark as Story* (Westminster Press, 1982)

J. Drury, *The Parables in the Gospels* (SPCK, 1985)

B. van Iersel, *Reading Mark* (T. & T. Clark, 1989)